STRENGTHENING YOUR MARRIAGE

WAYNE MACK

Formerly:
HOW TO DEVELOP DEEP UNITY IN THE MARRIAGE
RELATIONSHIP

PRESBYTERIAN AND REFORMED PUBLISHING CO.
Phillipsburg, New Jersey

Contents

Preface

In fulfillment of his doctoral program at Westminster Theological Seminary, Wayne Mack developed this outstanding practical volume. I have had the privilege and pleasure to monitor the efforts that he has put into the preparation of the material over the last two years, and I know that his work has been thorough. Beyond that, it is biblical.

Pastors, you will find that both the biblical studies and the personal exercises included will be useful to you in counseling with married couples in your church as well as in pre-marital counseling.

Surely, your own marriage can be strengthened, too. One way to begin to use this book is to work through it with your wife.

As you know, there are many books purporting to offer help in doing marriage counseling. And, as you also know quite well, there are only a few that deliver the goods. Usually what they provide is far less than that concrete, practical, how-to information that you really need to initiate and bring about scriptural change. This book is unique at this very point. You and your counselee (even on his own) can use it.

Dr. Mack has produced a volume to which you will turn again and again. Buy it; it belongs on your shelf!

JAY ADAMS
Dean of the Pastoral Institute
of Christian Counseling &
Educational Foundation
Laverock, Pennsylvania

Introduction

One plus one equals one may not be an accurate mathematical concept, but it is an accurate description of God's intention for the marriage relationship. That this is an accurate description of God's purpose for the marriage relationship is revealed in the creation account itself. Scripture says, "For this cause shall a man leave his father and mother and shall cleave to his wife, and they shall become *one flesh*" (Gen. 2:24).

Years of experience as a pastor and counselor have convinced me that many marriages are far below the biblical norm. Even many Christians are not experiencing the oneness in their marriages that God says they should have. These marriages are not providing the satisfaction that God intended them to bring. Nor are they the testimony for Christ that God wants them to be (Eph. 5:29-32).

This particular manual has been designed as a tool for developing true unity in the marriage relationship. The material is like a ladder or stairway, each unit being based upon and related to every other unit, with the goal of all the material being that of true unity or oneness in marriage.

Every unit has a teaching section which is presented in amplified outline form. Main points are italicized for the purpose of easy recognition and recall. Scripture references are given and it is hoped that you will study them to discover for yourself God's way of becoming truly one. Study questions and practical exercises also form a part of every unit. These study questions and exercises are not simply busy work. They are designed to provide the basis for practical, specific, personalized research and direction which will result in the development of greater unity in your marriage.

Scripture says, "In all labor there is profit" (Prov. 14:23), and nowhere is this more true than in the marriage relationship. Good, God-honoring marriages do not just happen. They are the result of dedicated, diligent, consistent prayer and work on the part of both husband and wife.

In this manual I call you to work—to work on the most important human relationship in your life. What I am going to ask you to do will not be easy. Time, effort, serious thought, painful examination, and honest evaluation will be required. But I guarantee you that your prayerful efforts will be richly rewarded.

Already the substance of this manual has been implemented by many people. The result has been that good marriages have been made better, sour marriages have become sweet, and God's name has been manifestly glorified. My hope and prayer is that our great God would use this manual to promote greater oneness in your marriage so that you may experience greater happiness and that His goodness, power, and glory may be more fully manifested.

Unity Through Understanding God's Purpose for Marriage

In this unit God's blueprint for marriage in Genesis 2:18-25 is considered. The concepts of leaving, cleaving, and becoming one flesh are presented and explained. Suggested reading and study questions to be completed by both the husband and the wife are included.

A. As far as I know there is only one statement about marriage that God includes four times in the Bible.

    1. He makes it in Genesis 2:24, Matthew 19:5, Mark 10:7, 8, and Ephesians 5:31. The statement is, "For this cause shall a man leave his father and mother and shall cleave to his wife, and they shall become one flesh."

    2. God makes this same statement about marriage four times.

        a. He make it once in the Old Testament and three times in the New Testament.

        b. He makes it once before man fell into sin and three times after man fell into sin.

    3. This statement contains God's marital purpose for perfect man and for sinful man. This statement contains God's all-time blueprint for a good marriage.

B. A good blueprint is just as necessary for a good marriage as it is for a building project.

    1. Today, there are many unhappy, unfulfilling marriages not only among non-Christians but also among Christians.

    2. This unhappiness is caused to a large extent by the failure of people to pay attention to God's blueprint for marriage.

    3. What then is God's blueprint for marriage? What does God's kind of marriage involve?

I. God's blueprint for marriage directs husbands and wives to leave their fathers and mothers.

A. What does it mean to leave your parents?

    1. Well, it certainly does not mean that you abandon or utterly forsake them. (Compare Exod. 21:12; Mark 7:9-13; I Tim. 5:8.)

    2. Nor does it mean that you must make a great geographical move. Living too close to parents at the beginning of a marriage may make it more difficult to leave, but it is possible to leave your father and mother and still live next door. Conversely, it is possible to live a thousand miles away from your parents and not leave them. In fact, you may not have left your parents even though they are dead.

1

B. To leave your parents means that your relationship to your parents must be radically changed.
   1. It means that you establish an adult relationship with them.
   2. It means that you must be more concerned about your mate's ideas, opinions, and practices than those of your parents.
   3. It means that you must not be slavishly dependent on your parents for affection, approval, assistance, and counsel.
   4. It means that you must eliminate any bad attitudes towards your parents, or you will be tied emotionally to them regardless of how far you move from them.
   5. It means that you must stop trying to change your mate simply because your parents do not like him the way he is.
   6. *It means that you make the husband and wife relationship your priority human relationship.*
      a. Yes, you should be concerned about being a good son/daughter —or mother/father, but you should be more concerned about being a good husband/wife than about being a good son/daughter or father/mother. *Children do not need indulgent parents who continually neglect each other. They need parents who will demonstrate how to face and solve problems.* They need parents who will show them how to be good husbands and wives; how to relate to other people.
      b. If you are parents, your goal should be to prepare your children to leave, not to stay. Your life must not be wrapped around them or you may make them emotional cripples.
      c. You should be preparing yourselves for the day when your children leave by cultivating common interests, by learning to do things together, and by deepening your friendship with each other.
      d. When your children have married, you must not try to run their lives. You must allow the young husband to be the head of his home, to make decisions for himself, to look to his wife, not you, as his primary responsibility and helper. You must encourage your daughter to depend upon her husband, not you, for guidance, help, companionship, and affection.
II. God's blueprint for marriage directs husbands and wives to cleave to one another.
   A. In our day many young couples seem to marry with the thought that if their marriage does not work out they can always get a divorce.
      1. When they marry, they vow to be faithful until death, but under their breath they add, "unless our problems are too great."
      2. Indeed, some suggest that we should renew our marriage license every year even as we do our automobile license. Others suggest

2

that we forget about the hassle of having to get a marriage license or going through a marriage ceremony.

3. For them, marriage is a matter of convenience, of chance, and may be very temporary. It all depends on how the cards fall out.

B. But God says, "No, that's not the way I planned it. I planned marriage to be a permanent relationship. I want the husband and wife to cleave to one another" (Mark 10:7-9).
1. Marriage, then, is not a matter of blind chance, but deliberate choice.
2. It is not merely a matter of convenience, but obedience.
3. It is not a matter of how the cards fall out, but of how much you are willing and determined to work at it.

C. A good marriage is based more on commitment than feeling or animal attraction.
1. According to Malachi 2:14 and Proverbs 2:17, marriage is an irrevocable covenant or contract to which we are bound.
2. Therefore, when two people get married they promise that they will be faithful to each other regardless of what happens.
   a. The wife promises that she will be faithful even if the husband is afflicted with bulges, baldness, bunions, and bifocals; even if he loses his health, his wealth, his job, his charm; even if someone more exciting comes along.
   b. The husband promises to be faithful even if the wife loses her beauty and appeal; even if she is not as neat and tidy or as submissive as he would like her to be; even if she does not satisfy his sexual desires completely; even if she spends money foolishly or is a terrible cook.
   c. Marriage means that a husband and wife enter into a relationship for which they accept full responsibility and in which they commit themselves to each other regardless of what problems arise.

D. In many ways getting married is like becoming a Christian.
1. When a person becomes a Christian he leaves his former way of life, his self-righteousness, his own efforts to save himself, and turns to Christ, who died in the place and stead of sinners.
2. In this act of turning to Christ, he commits himself to Christ. The very essence of saving faith is a personal commitment to Christ in which a person promises to trust Christ faithfully and completely and to serve Christ faithfully and diligently, regardless of how he feels or what problems arise. (Compare Rom. 10:9, 10; Acts 16:31; Phil. 3:7, 8; I Thess. 1:9, 10.)
3. Just so, *God's kind of marriage involves a total and irrevocable commitment of two people to each other.*
   a. God's kind of marriage involves cleaving to one another in sick-

ness and health, poverty and wealth, pleasure and pain, joy and sorrow, good times and bad times, agreements and disagreements.

    b. God's kind of marriage means that people know that they must face problems, discuss them, seek God's help in them, resolve them rather than run from them, because there is no way out. They are committed to one another for life. They must cleave to one another today and tomorrow, as long as they both shall live.

III. God's blueprint for marriage involves one flesh.

    A. At its most elementary level, this is referring to sexual relations or physical union.

        1. Consider I Corinthians 6:16.

        2. Within the bounds of marriage, sexual relations are holy, good, and beautiful, but if they are entered into apart from the "leaving and cleaving" they are ugly, degrading, and sinful. (Study Heb. 13:4.)

    B. But becoming one flesh involves more than the marriage act.

        1. Indeed, the marriage act is the symbol or culmination of a more complete oneness, of a total giving of yourself to another person. Consequently, if the more complete oneness is not a reality, sexual relations lose their meaning.

        2. One definition of marriage that I really like is: *Marriage is a total commitment and a total sharing of the total person with another person until death.*

            a. God's intention is that when two people get married they should share everything—their bodies, their possessions, their insights, their ideas, their abilities, their problems, their successes, their sufferings, their failures, etc.

            b. *A husband and wife are a team* and whatever each of them does must be for the sake of the other person, or at least it must not be to the detriment of the other person. Each must be *as* concerned about the other person's needs as he is about his own (Eph. 5:28; Prov. 31:12, 27).

            c. Husbands and wives are no more two, but one flesh. And this one flesh concept must manifest itself in practical, tangible, demonstrable ways. God does not intend it to be merely an abstract concept or idealistic theory, but a concrete reality. Total intimacy and deep unity are part of God's blueprint for a good marriage.

        3. Total intimacy and deep unity, however, do not mean total uniformity or sameness.

            a. My body is made up of many different parts. My hands do not do the work of my feet. My heart does not do the work of my liver.

b. There is great diversity in my body and yet there is unity. The parts of my body look different and even act differently, but when normal each part works for the benefit of the other parts, or at least one part does not deliberately try to hurt the other parts.

c. Similarly, husbands and wives may be very different in some respects, but they must not allow their differences to hinder their unity because God's purpose in marriage is total unity.

C. But you know as well as I do that total oneness is not easily achieved.

   1. Certainly the basic hindrance to the achievement of oneness is our sinfulness.

      a. In Genesis 2:25, immediately after God spoke of the husband/wife becoming one flesh, the Scripture says, "And the man and his wife were *both naked* and *were not ashamed.*"

      b. The nakedness of Adam and Eve is not a recommendation of public nudity. This happened before there were any other people around. Adam was the only human being who saw Eve naked, and Eve was the only person who saw Adam naked!

   2. And furthermore, this happened before they had sinned. After they sinned we read that "the eyes of them both were opened, and they knew that they were naked, and they sewed fig leaves together and made themselves loin coverings." As soon as sin entered the picture, they began to cover up.

      a. This attempt to cover up was certainly an evidence of their awareness of their sinfulness before God. Immediately and foolishly, they tried to hide their sin from God.

      b. Still further, this "covering up" symbolized an attempt to hide from each other. When sin entered the picture, their openness, transparency, and total oneness were destroyed.

   3. And just as sin entered and hindered the oneness of Adam and Eve, so our sinfulness is still the great barrier to marital oneness today.

      a. Sometimes marital oneness is destroyed by the sin of selfishness.

      b. Sometimes it is marred by the sin of pride.

      c. Sometimes it is broken by the sin of bitterness or ingratitude or stubbornness or unwholesome speech or neglect or impatience or harshness or cruelty.

      d. It was sin that destroyed the total oneness of Adam and Eve, and it is sin that destroys the oneness of husbands and wives today.

   4. *That brings us to our need of Jesus Christ.*

      a. First of all, *we need Jesus Christ to bring us into a right relationship with God.* (Compare Rom. 3:10-23; Isa. 59:2; Col. 1:

21-23; Eph. 1:7; 2:13-21; II Cor. 5:21; I Pet. 3:18.)

b. But *not only do we need Jesus Christ to bring us into a right relationship with God, we also need Jesus Christ to help us to be rightly related to each other.* Jesus Christ came into the world to destroy the barriers that exist between man and man as well as between man and God. He breaks down the barriers that exist between men. He abolishes the enmity and makes men one in Himself (Eph. 2:14-16; Gal. 3:28). He alone can take a sinful, selfish man and woman and enable them to leave father and mother, cleave to one another, and become one flesh.

c. If therefore you are going to experience the total oneness that God says is essential to a good marriage, you need to come to Jesus Christ. He breaks down barriers. He destroys middle walls that divide. He cleanses from sin. He breaks the power of reigning sin. He sets the prisoner free. He gives men the Holy Spirit, who produces in them the fruit of love, joy, peace, patience, kindness, goodness, faithfulness, gentleness, and self-control. He gives them the Holy Spirit, who enables sinful men and women to leave father and mother, to cleave to one another, and to become one flesh.

SUPPLEMENTARY READING FOR UNIT 1

Christian Living in the Home, Jay Adams, Presbyterian and Reformed Publishing Co., Nutley, N. J., 1973, chapter 4.

A Biblical View of the Sexes, Florence Brown, Christian Training Inc., Wilmington, Delaware, 1971, chapter 1.

The Family First, Kenneth Gangel, His International Service, Minneapolis, 1972, chapter 2.

The Christian Home in a Changing World, Gene Getz, Moody Press, Chicago, 1972, chapter 2.

Marriage Is for Love, Richard L. Strauss, Tyndale House Publishers, Wheaton, chapter 9.

God's Blueprint for Marriage
To be completed by husband and wife together.

A. Study Genesis 2:18-25.

1. Who originated the marriage institution? _____

2. What are the purposes of marriage? Why did God originate marriage? (Compare Gen. 1:28; 2:18; Eph. 5:22-32.)

   a. _____

   b. _____

   c. _____

   d. _____

3. In what ways is marriage "good"? (Gen. 2:18; Heb. 13:4).

   a. _____

   b. _____

4. What is a help-meet? _____

5. What does the word "help-meet" suggest about the man and the woman?

   a. The man _____

   b. The woman _____

6. According to Genesis 2:24, what is the primary human relationship in life?

   _____

7. What does leaving mother and father involve? _____

   _____

   _____

7

8. What do the words "shall cleave" suggest? _____

_____

_____

9. What do the words "they shall be one flesh" signify? _____

_____

_____

10. List some of the things that married people must do to promote and manifest this oneness.

    a. _____

    b. _____

    c. _____

    d. _____

    e. _____

    f. _____

    g. _____

    h. _____

11. What are some of the barriers to deep oneness?

    a. _____

    b. _____

    c. _____

    d. _____

    e. _____

    f. _____

g. _____

h. _____

12. Discuss your marriage in terms of leaving and cleaving and oneness.
    a. Have you really left your parents? In what ways is your marriage relationship being adversely affected because you are following your parents' example of handling stress, facing problems, reacting to people, etc.? Is your spouse the number one human being in your life? Ask him what he thinks.
    b. Are you really committed (cleaving) to your mate? How do you react to your mate's weaknesses, failures, needs, and problems? Does your treatment of your mate depend upon his performance? Must he earn your affection and approval? Ask him what he thinks.
    c. How would you rate the intimacy or sharing level of your marriage? Total? Partial? Very little? Is there anything you are afraid to share with each other? Do you think mostly in terms of "me" and "him" or "we"? Discuss the level of your spiritual, intellectual, emotional, sexual, recreational, financial, parental, communicational, occupational, aesthetic, and creative oneness. Where is your oneness weak, and where is it strong? How will you improve the weak areas?
13. Evaluate your own marriage. What do you like about your marriage as it is now? Strengths? What do you dislike? Weaknesses?

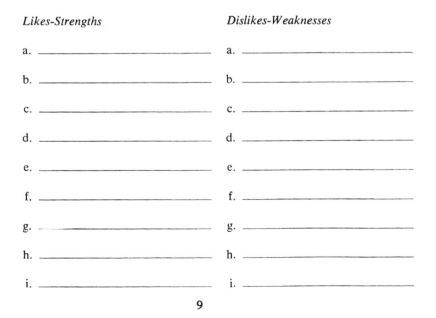

Likes-Strengths   *Dislikes-Weaknesses*

a. _____   a. _____

b. _____   b. _____

c. _____   c. _____

d. _____   d. _____

e. _____   e. _____

f. _____   f. _____

g. _____   g. _____

h. _____   h. _____

i. _____   i. _____

14. What are some worthwhile goals for your marriage?

   a. _____

   b. _____

   c. _____

   d. _____

   e. _____

   f. _____

   g. _____

15. Make a list of things that ought to be avoided if a good marriage relationship is to be maintained.

   a. _____

   b. _____

   c. _____

   d. _____

   e. _____

   f. _____

   g. _____

   h. _____

   i. _____

   j. _____

16. In one sentence (one word, if possible) describe your marriage.

_____

B. Study Matthew 5:31-32 and 19:1-9 to discover how permanent the marriage relationship is.
   1. What does Matthew 19:6 indicate about the permanency of the marriage relationship? _____

   _____

   2. Apart from death (Rom. 7:1-4), what do the aforementioned passages state as the only grounds for divorce? _____

   _____

   3. List several implications that emerge from the fact that marriage is a permanent relationship.

      a. _____

      b. _____

      c. _____

11

Unity Through a Clear Understanding of the Wife's Responsibilities

This unit promotes unity by explaining the way the wife is to complete or complement her husband. Suggested supplementary reading and study questions are included. The concept of aggressive submission is explored.

    A. *Most couples marry with high expectations for their marriage.*
        1. They know that many marriages have gone on the rocks, and many of those that did not are not really happy marriages. But they think their marriage will be different because they really love one another.
        2. So they begin marriage with great expectation, but often it is not long before the expectation is replaced with frustration. The marriage which they were sure was made in heaven comes crashing to the earth; the stars in their eyes become sand; the delight becomes disillusionment.
    B. *What happened?*
        1. Well, the two of them did not learn to conduct their personal lives or their marriage according to God's Word.
        2. When God created man and woman and ordained the marriage relationship, He was not like the inventor who invents a machine and then allows its purchaser to find out how the machine is to be used and operated, how the various parts are to relate to one another.
        3. No, God has provided specific information and direction concerning the purpose of marriage and the varying but complementary responsibilities of the two people who form the marriage. God has given certain responsibilities to the wife and certain responsibilities to the husband. *When two people know, accept, and fulfill their varying but complementary responsibilities, oneness in marriage is promoted.* Conversely, when the husband and wife either do not understand or will not fulfill their God-given responsibilities, great confusion and frustration will result.
    C. *At this point we will consider what God's Word has to say about the wife's primary responsibilities in marriage.* In the next unit we will consider the husband's responsibilities. (There are, of course, many passages in the Word of God which speak of the wife's part in marriage. Some of the key passages are Gen. 2:18-25; Prov. 31:10-31; Eph. 5: 22-24, 33; Titus 2:4, 5; I Pet. 3:1-6.)
  I. In the New Testament, the wife is frequently commanded to submit, to obey

12

or to be in subjection to her husband (Eph. 5:22-24, 33; Col. 3:18; Titus 2:4, 5; I Tim. 2:9-12; I Pet. 3:1-6).

A. The idea of the wife's submission is not a very popular one in our day. Sometimes antagonism to wifely submission arises out of sinful rebellion against the will of God. Sometimes, however, it may arise from a false picture of what the wife's submission involves. To correct this false picture, I want to state some things biblical submission is not.

1. *Submission is not merely a concept for women.* It is a concept for all believers. (Compare Eph. 5:21; Phil. 2:3, 4; I Pet. 5:5; Rom. 13:1; Heb. 13:17.)

2. *Submission does not mean that the wife becomes a slave.* Actually, the wife is never more free than when she is in submission to her husband, for then she is free to become all that God intended her to become. (Study the description of God's ideal wife in Prov. 31: 10-31.)

3. *Submission does not mean that the wife never opens her mouth, never has an opinion, never gives advice.* (Compare Prov. 31:26; Acts 18:26; Judges 13:21-23.)

4. *Submission does not mean that the wife becomes a wallflower who folds up and allows her abilities to lie dormant.* (Compare the full use that God's ideal wife made of her talents and abilities in Prov. 31.)

5. *Submission does not mean that the wife is inferior to the husband.* Jesus Christ was not inferior to Mary and Joseph, and yet the Scripture says that as a child, "He continued in subjection to them" (Luke 2:51). Jesus Christ was in no way inferior to God the Father. He was and is fully and completely God, in every sense. Yet the Scripture asserts that there is order and structure in the Trinity. Jesus said, "I can do nothing on my own initiative, as I hear I judge. . . . I do not seek my own will but the will of Him who sent me" (John 5:30), and Paul declared, "I want you to understand that Christ is the head of every man, and the man is the head of a woman and *God is the head of Christ"* (I Cor. 11:3). Certainly this does not imply that Christ is inferior to God the Father. Rather it teaches that there is a division of labor and responsibility in the Trinity. In like fashion, the submission of the wife in no way implies inferiority. Instead, it teaches the necessity for order and structure, for a division of responsibility within the home. Genesis 1:26, 27; 2:23; and Galatians 3:28 all assert the equalitarian status and dignity of women and men.

B. Having stated what the wife's submission does not mean, we will now look at submission from a more positive point of view.

1. *Scripture indicates that it is the wife's responsibility to make herself submissive.* Nowhere is the husband commanded to physically force

13

his wife into submission. Rather, the wife is commanded to make herself submissive. (Compare Eph. 5:22 and I Pet. 3:1.)

2. *Scripture indicates that the wife's submission is to be continuous.* The Greek verb in most passages about submission is in the present tense. Submission is to be the continuous life style of the wife. (Compare Eph. 5:22 and I Pet. 3:1.)

3. *Wifely submission is mandatory, not optional.* The Greek verb is in the imperative mood. (Compare Eph. 5:21, 22 and I Pet. 3:1.) Her submission is not to be based upon the way her husband treats her. Nor is it to be conditioned by the husband's abilities, talents, wisdom, education, or spiritual state. (Compare I Pet. 3:1 and Luke 2:51.)

4. *Wifely submission is a spiritual matter. It is to be done "as to the Lord"* (Eph. 5:22). *The Lord commands the wife to be submissive.* Refusal to submit to the husband is therefore rebellion against God Himself. Submission to the husband is a test of her love for God as well as a test of love for her husband. The wife then must look upon her submission to her husband as an act of obedience to Christ and not merely to her husband. Jesus said, "If you love me, you will keep my commandments" (John 14:15), and one of his commands to wives is, "Be subject to your own husbands . . ." (Eph. 5:22). *Still further, wifely submission is a spiritual matter because it must be performed in the power of the Holy Spirit.* The context in which submission is commanded indicates that it can be performed only by women whose hearts have been cleansed by the blood of Christ, by women who are being strengthened in the inner man by the Holy Spirit, by women who are being filled up to all fullness of God. (Compare Eph. 1:1–5:21; I Pet. 1:1–3:6.)

5. *Submission is a positive, not negative concept.* It emphasizes what the wife should do rather than what she should not do. In my opinion, Bill Gothard's definition of submission is right on target. He asserts that submission is "the freedom to be creative under divinely appointed authority." Submission means that the wife puts all of her talents, abilities, resources, energy at her husband's disposal. Submission means that the wife yields and uses all of her abilities under the management of her husband for the good of her husband and family. Submission means that she sees herself as a part of her husband's team. She is not her husband's opponent fighting at cross purposes or trying to outdo him. She is not merely an individual going her separate way. She is her husband's teammate striving for the same goal. She has ideas, opinions, desires, requests, and insights, and she lovingly makes them known. But she knows that on any good team someone has to make the final

14

decisions and plans. She knows that the team members must support the team leader, his plans and decisions, or no progress will be made, and confusion and frustration will result.

6. *Submission involves the wife's attitudes as well as her actions.* Jesus Christ was thoroughly submitted to the Father. He said, "My food is to do the will of Him who sent me and to accomplish His work" (John 4:34). But how did He serve the Father? In a spirit of resignation, servility, or heaviness? No, He served the Father with gladness. He delighted to do the Father's will (Ps. 40:7, 8). Likewise, the wife's submission to her husband is to be cheerful, not servile or grudging.

Scripture declares that God's kind of wife "works with her hands in delight" (Prov. 31:13), finding great satisfaction in using all of her God-given resources to fulfill the needs of her husband and family. Ephesians 5:33 contains a very important injunction concerning the attitude in which a wife should submit to her husband. It says, "Let the wife see to it that she respect her husband." As she submits to her husband, she is to do so with respectful attitude. What this means is clarified by the Amplified Version of the New Testament when it asserts that the wife is to notice, regard, honor, prefer, esteem, praise, and admire her husband exceedingly.

7. *Wifely submission is to be extensive.* She is to be subject unto her husband *as* the church is to Christ (Eph. 5:24). And how broad should the submission of the church be to Christ? Well, the submission of the church to Christ is to be total; it is to be comprehensive. Christ is "head over all things for the church" (Eph. 1:22), and the church is to do whatever it does in word or deed in the name of the Lord Jesus, in total dependence upon His person, acknowledging and recognizing Him in all its ways, doing all for His honor and glory (Col. 3:17; Prov. 3:5, 6; I Cor. 10:31).

In like fashion Paul says, "the wives are to be subject to their husbands in *everything.*" Submission is not to be an on-again off-again matter for the wife. Nor is it to be a selective, choose what you like, reject what you do not like proposition. Submission is to be her life style at all times, in all places, and in everything.

Certainly this does not mean that she must obey her husband when he commands her to do what God forbids or tries to keep her from doing what God commands. She is to be subject to her husband *"as is fitting in the Lord"* (Col. 3:18). Her husband's authority is a delegated or ministerial authority. He has authority because he is under the authority of God. As long as he does not ask her to do what God forbids or forbids her from doing what God commands,

15

she is to submit. Failure to do so would be rebellion against God as well as her husband. However, since her husband's authority is delegated to him, he loses his authority at those times and in those areas when his directives are *clearly* contrary to the revealed will of God as it is found in the Bible. When the husband asks her to do that which is unmistakably contrary to the Word of God, the wife must obey God rather than man (Acts 5:28 29).

The wife's submission to her husband then is to be extensive but not necessarily total or unlimited. She is to obey him in everything except that which contradicts the Word of God. And even then she is to disobey in a loving, submissive fashion, explaining calmly and clearly her reasons for disobedience, assuring her husband of her love and loyalty, and seeking to demonstrate that love and loyalty in a variety of continuous and tangible ways. She is to be her husband's helper (Gen. 2:18), and this she can never be if she manifests a contentious, inconsiderate, uncooperative spirit.

II. An honest examination of scriptural data leads to the conclusion that the wife's primary ministry in life is her husband. When God created Eve for Adam He said, "It is not good for the man to be alone; I will make him a helper suitable [literally, corresponding to] for him. And out of the ground the Lord formed every beast of the field and every bird of the sky. . . . But for Adam there was not found a helper suitable for him. So the Lord God caused a deep sleep to fall upon the man, and he slept; then He took one of the ribs and closed up the flesh at that place. And the Lord God fashioned into a woman the rib which He had taken from the man, and brought her to the man" (Gen. 2:18-22).

A. Several important facts about the wife's relationship to her husband emerge from this passage.

1. *God made the woman to be man's helper.* Without the woman, man, even in his perfect condition, was incomplete.

2. *God made the woman to be a suitable helper.* None of the animals could provide the kind of help that man needed. Only woman could do that. "He who finds a wife finds a good thing, and obtains favor from the Lord" (Prov. 18:22). "An excellent wife, who can find? For her worth is far above jewels. The heart of her husband trusts in her, and he will have no lack of gain" (Prov. 31:10, 11).

3. *God created the woman to correspond to man.* She is similar to man, yet somewhat different. She is man's complement, not his carbon copy. She is to man what a key is to a lock and what a film is to a camera—indispensable (I Cor. 11:11).

B. According to the Scripture the wife was made to fulfill the needs, the lacks, the inadequacies of her husband. She was made to be *her hus-*

16

band's unique helper. She is to *"do him good* and not evil all the days of her life" (Prov. 31:12). She is to be like *a fruitful vine* in her husband's house (Ps. 128:3). She is to be "one flesh" with her husband, and this will happen only as she accepts and fulfills her God-appointed role in marriage.

1. *This does not mean that everything she does must have a direct connection to her husband.* Nor does it mean that she should never do anything for her own benefit or for the benefit of others, or that she should never become involved in activities or ministries outside the home (Prov. 31:10-31).

2. *It does mean, however, that she ought never to do anything which would be detrimental or harmful to her husband* or that would cause her to neglect her primary ministry of helping her husband (Prov. 31:10-31).

C. And now becoming very specific, I want to suggest some ways in which a wife may help her husband. She may help her husband by:

1. *Making the home a safe place*—a place of encouragement, comfort, understanding and refuge (Prov. 31:11, 20). Do not use jokes about him or make cutting remarks to him. Do not constantly remind him of his faults, mistakes, and failures. Correct him only if it is absolutely necessary. Avoid the danger of allowing the home to be in shambles and full of disorder and confusion. But also avoid the danger of making the house a show place where everything must always be neat and immaculate. Husbands want homes to live in, not show places to visit.

2. *Being trustworthy and dependable* (Prov. 31:11, 12).

3. *Maintaining a good attitude* (Prov. 31:26, 28, 29; James 3:13-18; Phil. 4:4).

4. *Discussing things lovingly, openly, and honestly* (Eph. 4:25).

5. *Being satisfied* with her position, her possessions, her tasks (Phil. 4:6-13; Heb. 13:5, 16).

6. *Being longsuffering, forgiving, and forbearing* (Eph. 4:2, 31, 32; Col. 3:12-14).

7. *Showing an interest in his problems and concerns* (Phil. 2:3, 4).

8. *Being an industrious, frugal, diligent, ambitious, and creative member of the team* (Ps. 128:3; Prov. 31:10-31).

9. *Offering suggestions, advice, and corrections when needed in a loving fashion* (Prov. 31:26).

10. *Keeping herself beautiful, especially in the inner person* (I Pet. 3:3-5).

11. *Maintaining a good spiritual life* (I Pet. 3:1, 2, 7).

12. *Cooperating with him in raising children* (Eph. 6:20; Prov. 31:26-28; I Tim. 5:13, 14).

17

*13. *Building loyalty to him in the children.* The wife's attitudes toward the husband are quickly picked up by the children. Lack of respect or confidence in his leadership, complaints about what he has or has not done will have debilitating influence on the children. She must avoid taking sides with the children or anyone against her husband. She must support and cooperate with him in discipline. All differences of opinion about discipline should be settled away from the children.

*14. *Being grateful to him.* Appreciation should be expressed freely and in a variety of ways (Rom. 13:7).

*15. *Showing confidence in his decisions.* Disdain, lack of confidence, anxiety, or strong opposition over his decisions may cause him to become indecisive, defensive, or reactionary. If the wife doubts the wisdom of important decisions, she should ask questions in a non-threatening way, assuming that there are some facts she does not know and that he really does want what is best for them both (I Cor. 13:4-8).

D. Wives, God calls you to be in submission to your husband, to be his unique and suitable helper.

   1. To some extent in this unit we have seen what that means.

   2. But knowing what it means is of little value, unless it is applied to your relationship with your husband. Knowing these facts will not promote oneness in marriage. Performing them will.

   3. I ask you wives to examine your relationship to your husbands in the light of these truths. Are you really practicing submission to your husband? Are you really his helper? I suggest that where you find yourself to be failing:

     a. Make confession of your sin to God and your husband.

     b. Seek cleansing from this sin and all your sins through the blood of Christ (Eph. 1:7; I John 1:9).

     c. Ask the Holy Spirit for power to be different (Gal. 5:16,22,23).

     d. Move out in obedience to the Word of God, and make the necessary changes (Phil. 2:12, 13; James 1:19-24).

---

*(Grateful acknowledgment for the substance of suggestions 13-15 is given to Robert D. Smith, M.D. Dr. Smith has granted permission for their inclusion. He indicates that his remarks are a distillation of concepts taught by Bill Gothard.)

SUPPLEMENTARY READING FOR UNIT 2

Christian Living in the Home, Jay Adams, chapter 6.

The Christian Family, Larry Christenson, Bethany Fellowship, Minneapolis, 1970, chapter 2.

The Christian Home in a Changing World, Gene Getz, chapter 4.

The Christian Home, Shirley Rice, Norfolk Christian Schools, Norfolk, 1967, lessons 5 and 6.

Discovering the Intimate Marriage, R. C. Sproul, Bethany Fellowship, Minneapolis, 1975, chapter 3.

Marriage Is for Love, Richard L. Strauss, chapter 9.

Christ in the Home, Robert Taylor, Jr., Baker Book House, Grand Rapids, 1973, chapters 7 and 8.

DISCUSSION AND STUDY QUESTIONS FOR UNIT 2

Role of Wife
To be completed by husband and wife together.

A. Study Ephesians 5:22-33 and answer the following questions.

1. What is the one word that summarizes the wife's responsibility to the husband? Compare also I Peter 3:1 and I Timothy 2:9-12.

_____

_____

2. What do the words "as unto the Lord" (vs. 22) suggest about the wife's submission?

_____

_____

3. According to verse 24, how extensive should a woman's submission be?

_____

_____

4. What limit is put upon the wife's submission by Colossians 3:18 and Acts 5:29?

_____

_____

19

5. According to verse 24, what does the wife's relationship to her husband involve?

_____

_____

_____

6. According to verse 33, what should the wife's attitude be to her husband? What does this mean? Give several specific examples of what this would mean in practice.

_____

_____

_____

7. What does the wife's submission involve? Does it mean that she is inferior to her husband? Does it stifle her initiative and cause her to neglect her abilities? Study Proverbs 31:10-31 to answer these questions. Make a list of the ways that the virtuous woman of Proverbs 31 does use her abilities.

a. _____

b. _____

c. _____

d. _____

e. _____

f. _____

g. _____

h. _____

i. _____

j. _____

k. _____

l. _____

m. _____

n. _____

o. _____

8. Formulate a biblical definition of what the wife's submission means.

_____

_____

9. How can you express submission to your husband in the following areas?

a. Housework _____

_____

b. Sexual relations _____

_____

c. Social relations _____

_____

d. Child discipline _____

_____

e. Husband's work _____

_____

f. Meal preparation _____

_____

g. Family devotions _____

_____

21

h. Church life _____

_____

B. List your personal habits which annoy your husband. Begin to work on correcting them unless to do so would contradict the Bible.

1. _____

2. _____

3. _____

4. _____

5. _____

6. _____

7. _____

8. _____

C. List ways by which you can remind, correct, or advise your husband without being bossy or nagging.

1. _____

2. _____

3. _____

4. _____

5. _____

6. _____

7. _____

8. _____

D. Discuss the various ways in which you are completing and complementing your husband; ways in which you are your husband's helper; ways in which you are doing your husband "good."

1. _____

2. _____

3. _____

4. _____

5. _____

6. _____

7. _____

8. _____

E. Discuss other ways that you could or should complete or complement him. Does he have needs which you could be fulfilling but are not? How can you help your husband more than you now are?

1. _____

2. _____

3. _____

4. _____

5. _____

6. _____

7. _____

8. _____

F. Discuss ways in which you may be competing with your husband instead of completing him. Are you trying to outdo or at least equal your husband? Are you trying to be a duplicate of your husband? Are you trying to be a lock when God made you to be a key?

1. _____

2. _____

3. _____

4. _____

5. _____

6. _____

7. _____

8. _____

G. What could you do to strengthen your marriage relationship?

1. _____

2. _____

3. _____

4. _____

5. _____

6. _____

7. _____

8. _____

9. _____

10. _____

H. Make a list of ways in which you could or do let your husband know he is important to you. How do you show respect for your husband?

1. _____

2. _____

3. _____

4. _____

5. _____

6. _____

7. _____

8. _____

9. _____

10. _____

Unity Developed Through a Clear Understanding of the Husband's Responsibilities

This unit deals with the other half of the coin, showing how the husband must complete his wife. Oneness can be achieved only as the husband knows and fulfills his biblical role. Biblical principles concerning the husband's responsibilities to his wife are enunciated. Suggested supplementary reading and study questions are included. The concept of the husband as a servant-leader is explained.

A. *Genuine unity requires a sorting out of responsibilities.*

1. Imagine the confusion that would occur on a football team where no one knew his specific responsibility.

2. Imagine the frustration that would exist in a business where there were no job descriptions, where everything was everybody's business and nothing was anybody's business, where everyone was a "chief" and no one was an "Indian."

3. Well, that is the kind of confusion and frustration that does exist in many marriages because there has never been a sorting out of the responsibilities. Everyone is a "chief" and no one is an "Indian."

B. *Real oneness cannot be experienced unless the husband and wife know, accept, and fulfill their varying but complementary responsibilities.*

1. In Unit 2, we considered the wife's *God-given responsibilities* to her husband. In this unit we will consider the other side of the coin, or *the husband's God-given responsibilities to his wife.*

2. What I was concerned about in the last unit was God's declaration of the wife's responsibilities, and what I am concerned about in this unit is God's declaration of the husband's responsibilities.

   a. I am interested in what society has to say about these matters.

   b. But I am even more concerned about what God has to say:

   1) Because I am a Christian.

   2) Because I know that the God who made the woman and man is far wiser than they are.

   3) And because I know that God's commandments are not burdensome. His will is "good, well pleasing and perfect." If God gives to the woman certain responsibilities, they are good and well pleasing for her. If God gives to the man certain responsibilities, He does so for good and wise reasons. And the man or woman who fights with God's declaration of responsibility is doing a very foolish thing, for that person

is denying himself the privilege of experiencing genuine oneness in the marriage relationship.

C. *There are, of course, many passages in the Bible which speak of the man's part in marriage.*

    1. Some of the key passages are Genesis 3:16; Ephesians 5:23-33; I Timothy 3:4, 5; Psalm 128; I Peter 3:7; I Corinthians 7:3, 4; Proverbs 5:15-19; Colossians 3:19.

    2. As I read these passages I hear God saying that the husband has two primary responsibilities to his wife.

        a. He is to be his wife's leader.

        b. He is to be his wife's lover.

I. *The husband is to be his wife's leader* (Eph. 5:23; I Tim. 3:4, 5, 12; I Cor. 11:3).

A. Today, when we speak of leadership, the first thing that comes to mind is an idea about giving orders and being a boss.

    1. But this is not the first thing that should come to mind if we are thinking biblically.

        a. Matthew 20:20-28 gives us the Bible's concept of a leader. According to this passage, *a leader is first and foremost a servant.* His concern is not for himself; his concern is not to give orders, to boss other people around, to have his own way. His concern is to meet the needs of others. Indeed, if the best interests of others are not on his heart, if he is not willing to sacrifice himself—his personal needs, wants, desires, aspirations, time, money—if the needs of others are not more important than his own, he is not qualified to lead.

        b. John 13:1-15 gives us the same picture of what it means to be a leader. In this passage, the emblem of leadership is not a throne or a club but a big towel and a basin. In other words, a leader must have a servant's heart. And if he has a servant's heart, he will act like a servant and react like a servant when he is treated like a servant. (Note how I Pet. 5:3 and II Thess. 2:5-11 illustrate the same concept.)

    1. When we apply this biblical concept of leadership to the husband, we see that *being the leader means that he must be the family's biggest servant.*

        a. He is to be the head of his wife *even as* Christ is the head of the church (Eph. 5:23).

        b. His great model in leadership is Jesus Christ, who made Himself a servant (Phil. 2:6-8); who came not to be served, but to serve, and to give His life a ransom for many (Mark 10:45); who is head over all things for the sake of the church (Eph. 1:22, 23). Whatever Jesus Christ does, He does for our sake;

He does with our best interests at heart.

    c. In similar fashion, *the husband is to live for the sake of his wife, always keeping her best interests at heart.* He is to be his wife's servant-leader.

B. Having established the fact that biblical leadership requires a servant's heart, I want to point out some of the specific ways in which Jesus Christ, the great leadership model, led His disciples.

    1. *Jesus Christ practiced the principle of continuous association with those whom He led.*

        a. He did not lead His disciples by long distance telephone calls, or by writing them a few letters or by infrequent visits. For over three years, He spent great amounts of time with them. (Compare John 1:39, 43; Mark 1:17; 3:14; 4:10; 5:1, 30, 31, 40; 6:1, 30, 31, 32, 35; 8:1, 10, 27, 34; 9:2, 30; 10:13, 23, 46; 11:1.)

        b. *Biblical leadership requires association with those who are being led.* Significantly, Peter commands husbands to *dwell* or *live* with their wives (I Pet. 3:7). No husband is fulfilling his God-given responsibility to his wife who does not delight in and arrange for frequent and regular companionship with her. (Note the same word used in Col. 3:16 and Eph. 3:17. What the Christian is to do with the Word of Christ in his heart, the husband is to do with his wife in the home.)

    2. *Jesus Christ carefully and relevantly instructed His disciples.*

        a. In many places Scripture asserts that Jesus taught His disciples. (Compare Matt. 5:1; Mark 4:10; John 13–16.) In fact, *the word "teacher" was one of the titles by which Jesus was frequently called* (John 3:2; 13:13).

        b. Sometimes He taught His disciples in a formal way (Matt. 5:1, 2; John 13–16). On other occasions He taught them in an informal way, in the midst of life situations, when He was faced by a crisis or confrontation, or when He was asked a question (Matt. 19:3-12, 16-27; 21:12-32).

        c. But whether He taught them in a formal or informal way, it is an established fact that Jesus Christ led and served His disciples by teaching them.

        d. Undoubtedly, God also expects the husband to lead and serve his wife by teaching her. (Note I Cor. 14:35, where the role of the husband as the wife's teacher is clearly established.)

    3. *Jesus Christ led His disciples by being a good example.*

        a. Frequently as we read the Gospels, we hear Jesus saying, "Follow me," or "Come after me," or "I have left you an example." He did not simply tell men that they ought always to pray.

He lived a life of constant prayer. He did not merely tell men to believe in the sovereignty of God. He lived a life that manifested confidence in and submission to the sovereignty of God. He did not merely preach to men that the Scriptures should be their final authority. He lived a life which was an example of what it means to make the Scriptures the final authority in your life. His life then was an example in living color of what He wanted His disciples to believe and how He wanted them to live. On the one hand, His exemplary life was a pattern or model for His disciples to follow. On the other hand, it earned their respect and made them willing to submit to His authority and leadership. (Compare also Phil. 4:9; I Thess. 2:7-10; I Pet. 5:3.)

b. Surely biblical leadership involves being an example for those who are being led. Surely the husband's leadership means that he must strive to be an example, a model, a pattern of godliness, holiness, compassion, dedication, and devotion to God.

c. Certainly, because of his remaining sinfulness, no earthly husband will ever be a perfect example for his wife, but that is what he should strive for (Phil. 3:12-14). And when he fails, he should be quick to confess to his God and his wife that he has failed and ask for forgiveness. Even in failure, the husband must be an example to his wife of how the believer should deal with sin. In failure, as well as at all other times, the Christian husband is to lead his wife by the power and authority of a good example.

4. *Jesus Christ led His disciples by making decisions and delegating responsibility to them.*

a. Compare John 4:1, 2; Mark 1:35-39; 6:7; 6:35-43; John 11:39-44; Matt. 10:1-14; 16:21-23; 21:1, 2; 28:18-20, where Jesus made decisions and delegated responsibilities to His disciples.

b. Note that when Jesus delegated He gave clear, concise, and specific directions so that the disciples knew what was expected of them and how they should go about their tasks.

c. At the same time, Scripture makes it clear that He gave them room to use their own initiative and creativity. He also was sensitive to their fears, needs, questions, spiritual, emotional, and physical state. He gave them a basic structure in which to work but a large measure of freedom within that structure.

d. Similarly, Christian husbands are called upon to lead their wives by making decisions and by delegating responsibility. To be the leader does not mean that he must bear all the re-

29

sponsibility and do all the work while his wife bears nothing and does nothing. It does mean that he will see to it that the work gets done and that everyone knows who does what.

    e. Husbands are supposed to lead, and leading involves making decisions and delegating responsibility. Any organization where only two people are involved needs someone who is final authority, or chaos and confusion will result. Fifty-fifty marriages are an impossibility. They do not work. They cannot work. *In marriage someone has to be the final decision maker.* Someone has to delegate responsibility, and *God has ordained that this should be the husband.* Indeed, the husbands must make decisions and delegate responsibility as a servant of his wife. Her opinions, advice, desires, suggestions, requests, fears, and questions should be given serious consideration. The wife is to be the husband's helper. She is to be his chief adviser, resource person, and consultant.

        In fact, if the wife's opinion differs from the husband's *on major issues* where there is no scriptural directive, I think the husband should be very careful about forcing his opinion upon the wife. Perhaps at these times, the best course of action for the husband would be to assure his wife that he respects her opinion and ask her to pray with him for a clearer understanding of what God wants them to do.

        At the same time, while being very sensitive to his wife, the husband must not become indecisive or fearful about making decisions and delegating responsibilities. Nor must he relinquish his decision making, delegating responsibility to his wife. At times, he may decide to allow his wife to make decisions (e.g., where they will go on vacation, what rugs or drapes or furniture they will buy), but he must never relinquish his overall decision-making responsibility. God has called him to be his wife's leader, and he cannot be her leader by being her follower.

C. Husbands, God calls you to be your wife's leader.

    1. This means that you must be your wife's servant, that you must spend much time with her, that you must give her useful, scriptural, and practical instruction, that you must be a good example to her, and that you must make decisions and delegate responsibilities in your home.

    2. Of the many elements involved in developing genuine oneness, none is more important than this one. Unquestionably, it is the other side of the marital coin. If genuine oneness is to be experienced, the lifestyle of the wife must be genuine biblical submis-

sion. Conversely, the lifestyle of the husband must be the kind of leadership that has just been described.

II. But the Bible not only says that the husband must be his wife's leader, it also asserts that he is to be his wife's lover.

    A. Dr. Jay Adams, author, counselor, seminary professor, has combined these two concepts and said that in the home the husband is to provide loving leadership.

        1. *The husband is not only to be a leader, he is to be a loving leader.* The importance of husbandly love has already been implied in what has previously been said about the husband, but now it must be emphasized and amplified.

        2. *The wife has such a great need for love or the husband has such a great lack of love, that God commands the husband to love his wife three times within the space of a few verses* in Ephesians 5.

            a. Two times in this passage God enjoins the husband to *love his wife even as he loves himself* (vss. 28, 33).

            b. One time God instructs the husband to *love his wife just as Christ also loved the church* (vs. 25).

    B. Oceans of truth concerning the husband's relationship to his wife are opened to us by these verses.

        1. *Normally, a man uses a lot of time and gives a great deal of thought, effort, and money to take care of himself.*

            a. His needs, his desires, his aspirations, his hopes, his body, his comfort are very important to him. He nourishes and cherishes himself. He carefully protects and provides for the needs of his body. He does not deliberately do that which would bring harm to himself. When he is hungry, he eats. When he is thirsty, he drinks. When he is tired, he sleeps. When he is in pain, he goes to the doctor. When he cuts himself, he washes the wound and binds it up. When he sees an object coming toward him, he puts up his hands for protection. He very naturally and carefully and fervently nourishes and cherishes himself.

            b. "Well," the Scripture indicates, "this is the way a man is to love his wife. He is to nourish her, cherish her, protect her, satisfy her, provide for her, care for her, sacrifice for her to the same degree and extent, and in the same manner as he does himself."

            c. Now that is a lot of love that a husband is to have for his wife. That is a high standard for a husband to keep, but there is still a higher standard.

        2. *Scripture says, "Husbands, love your wives just as Christ also loved the church."*

a. Who of us fully understands the love that Christ has for the church? Scripture speaks of the breadth and length and height and depth of the love of Christ which surpasses knowledge (Eph. 3:18, 19). Of this great love, Samuel Francis wrote, "Oh the deep, deep love of Jesus, vast, unmeasured, boundless, free, rolling as a mighty ocean, in its fullness over me."

b. *Who then can understand, who then can plumb the depths of the love of Jesus for His people?* No one! "We may sound the depths of all the mighty oceans, We may tell the distance to the farthest star; But the mighty love of God cannot be measured. Its dimensions are so high, so deep, so far." (First stanza of a song by John Peterson and Alfred Smith.)

c. *But this much we do know about love of Christ for His people.*
   1) *It is an unconditional or free love* (Rom. 5:8).
   2) *It is a volitional love.* He chooses to love us (Deut. 7:7; Eph. 1:6, 7).
   3) *It is an intense love* (John 13:1; Eph. 5:2, 25).
   4) *It is an unending love* (John 13:1; Jer. 31:3; Rom. 8:39).
   5) *It is an unselfish love* (Phil. 2:6, 7).
   6) *It is a purposeful love.* He works for our improvement, our development, our happiness, our welfare (Eph. 5:26, 27).
   7) *It is a sacrificial love.* He loved us and gave himself for us. He died, the just for the unjust, to bring us to God. In love, He endured the horrible death of the cross with all of its physical and spiritual torture and agony. In love, He bore the guilt and penalty of sin and the wrath of God in the place of His people. In love, He personally bore our sins in His own body on the cross so that the penalty and power and devastating effects of sin in our lives might be broken (Eph. 5:2, 25; Gal. 2:20; I Pet. 3:18; Rom. 5:6-11; I Pet. 2:24).
   8) *It is a manifested love.* Christ manifests His love in words and deeds. He tells us He loves us. He shows us He loves us. He protects us, prays for us, guards us, strengthens us, helps us, defends us, teaches us, comforts us, chastens us, equips us, empathizes with us, and provides for all our needs (John 10:1-14; 14:1-3; 13:34, 35; 15:9-10; Rom. 8:32; Phil. 4:13, 19; Heb. 4:14-16).

3. *This then is the standard by which a husband is to judge his relationship with his wife.*
   a. No husband has ever fully loved his wife in that way or to that degree or extent.
   b. But it is the goal toward which every husband is to press; the model which he is to follow.

c. And surely every husband ought to spend much time thinking about what this means in terms of his marital relationship. Certainly every husband should frequently examine himself to see where he is failing to be the lover his wife needs and God commands him to be.

d. Is he really loving his wife as he loves himself? Is he really pressing toward the goal of loving his wife as Christ loved the church? Is his love for his wife unconditional, volitional, intensive, unending, unselfish, purposeful, and sacrificial? Is his love being manifested in numerous and continuous ways? These are questions that every husband should be asking himself and perhaps his wife about himself.

4. Earlier in this manual, I said that the wife seems to have a great need for love and the husband seems to have a great lack of love.

a. *When it comes to being the lover God wants us to be, most of us do not reach first base.* We like to think that we are great lovers, but in reality we are very unperceptive.

b. Perhaps this is why Scripture admonishes husbands to dwell with their wives in an understanding way or according to knowledge. Maybe it is because we husbands do not give our wives and our relationship to them enough consideration that God gives this command to us in I Peter 3:7.

C. What does it mean in practical terms to live with your wife in an understanding way? How can a husband communicate his love to his wife? Well, let me suggest a few ways in which you as a husband may love your wife.

1. *One of the simplest, yet most neglected, ways of communicating love is by way of words.*

a. Some husbands treat the words "I love you" as though they were dirty words and almost never speak them.

b. Other husbands treat them as though they were rare pieces of china, using them only on special occasions or when asked by the wife, "Do you love me?"

c. Actually, these are words that should be commonly heard around your home. Most women crave verbal assurance of their husbands' love.

2. *You may love your wife by providing for the satisfaction of her varying needs* (I Tim. 5:8; I John 3:17; Eph. 5:28). Remember, your wife has a variety of needs. She has physical, emotional, intellectual, social, recreational, sexual, and spiritual needs. And you are not a good provider or lover if you are not concerned about all of them.

3. *You may love your wife by protecting her* (Eph. 5:28).

a. Your wife needs physical protection. She may be trying to do more than she is physically capable of doing.
b. The demands of carrying children or caring for children may be destroying her. The criticisms or expectations of others may be overwhelming her.
c. She may need protection in many different ways, and you can show your love to her by being her great protector.

4. *You may express love to your wife by assisting her to fulfill her chores and responsibilities.*
    a. Sometimes husbands think that there is something unmasculine about doing the dishes, cleaning the house, taking care of the children, or going shopping.
    b. Some husbands will not lift a finger to do anything they consider to be "women's work." He can be in a room where the baby begins to cry, and the wife can be at the other end of the house, but the husband will not find out why the baby is crying. Instead, he calls, "Jane, the baby is crying. Come here and do something about it." And she has to drop what she is doing and come all the way to where he is. Well, if this type of thing happens in enough instances, she begins to think, "My husband does not really love me. Oh, he says he does. But he really does not because if he did he would be willing to help me."

5. *You may express your love by sacrificing for her* (Eph. 5:25; Phil. 2:5, 6).
    a. Perhaps you come home from work all tired out. You want to plop down in your chair and read the newspaper, watch television, or read a book. Your wife, however, has other ideas. She wants to talk. Or she wants to go out to eat and then do some shopping. And she wants you to go with her.
    b. At that point, if you deny yourself and do what she wants to do, even though it is the opposite of what you want to do, you will be saying "I love you" to her in a very loud voice.

6. *You may love your wife by allowing her really to share your life* (I Pet. 3:7—"heirs together of the grace of life").
    a. Some time ago I counseled with a couple whose marriage was in deep trouble. As I talked to them I discovered that the wife felt shut out of her husband's life. She knew almost nothing about him, his past, his inner feelings, his hopes, his dreams. She felt like she was living with a stranger because her husband would not open up. She had great difficulty in believing that he really cared, that he really loved her.
    b. Put in the same circumstances, most women would be tempted to think the same way. Generally speaking, the more a hus-

band shares with his wife, the more he opens up to her, the more she gets the message from him that he cares, that he loves her.

7. *You may express your love by refusing to compare her unfavorably with other people, especially other women.*
   a. Husbands often point out some ability she lacks or some characteristic, quality, or feature they prefer.
   b. Their intention may be to challenge their wives to make some change or try to improve, but the wife takes it as a "put down." The wife thinks that the other person pleases the husband more or is more important and attractive to him than she is.

8. *You may express your love by demonstrating to her that, apart from your relationship to Jesus Christ, she has first place in your life.*
   a. She needs to know that she comes before your business, your children, your parents, your house, your hobbies, your golf game. She needs to know that, apart from Christ, you delight in her more than anything or anyone else.
   b. If she knows that, she will be secure. She will know you love her. If she does not, she may doubt your love.
   c. Now it is easy for us to say, "Apart from Christ, my wife is first in my life." But each husband needs to examine himself to see if she really is. To help you to determine whether your wife has first place or not, ask yourself the following questions. *What means more to me:* My wife or my children? Talking with my wife or having sex with her? Meeting my wants or satisfying her needs? Praying with my wife or with other people? Helping others or helping my wife? My work or my family? My church activities or my family's needs? Talking to other people or my wife? Having the appreciation of others or the appreciation of my wife? The opinions and ideas of others or the opinions and ideas of my wife?

9. *You may express your love by giving her a lot of tenderness, respect, chivalry, and courtesy* (Eph. 5:28; Col. 3:19; I Cor. 13:4, 5).
   *a. Do not use jokes about her or make cutting remarks to her in front of other people. If she makes a mistake, misquotes someone or does or says something that makes her look foolish to others, tell her about it privately. And do that only if her mistake will have harmful results for someone.
   b. *Speak to her in a gentle and respectful way.* Be a gentleman. do not use harsh words or rough speech.
   c. *Treat her as you would a valuable jewel rather than a piece of cinder or a garbage can.* Treat her as you would an expensive, useful, sensitive instrument rather than a cheap, useless, indestructible tool.

10. *You may love her by expressing appreciation and praise generously and in large doses* (I Pet. 3:7; Prov. 31:28).
*a. Be very careful to observe her attempts to please you.
b. Never laugh at or belittle the little things she may do for you.
c. Express appreciation and respect for her insights, ideas, questions, prayers, character, opinions, and fellowship as well as for her cooking and cleaning and satisfying your physical needs.
d. Men are often very short on expressing praise and appreciation to and for their wives. One helpful way of overcoming this tendency is to make a list of 90 to 100 things that you appreciate about your wife. When you have made this list, think of the many ways you may express appreciation, and go to work. Do your utmost to make your wife think that she is the most appreciated and loved woman in the world.

III. Conclusion.
A. *Husbands, God calls you to be your wife's leader and lover.*
1. To some extent we have seen what that means.
2. But knowing what it means is of little value unless it is applied to your relationship with your wife. Knowing these facts will not promote oneness in marriage. Performing them will.
B. I ask you, therefore, to *seriously examine your relationship with your wife* in the light of these truths.
1. Look back over what we have seen about your responsibility to be your wife's leader and lover.
2. Specifically note areas where you are failing and where you should improve.
3. When you have identified those areas:
a. *Make confession of your sin to God and to your wife* (I John 1:9; Matt. 5:23, 24; James 5:16).
b. *Seek cleansing from this sin and all your sins through the blood of Christ* (Eph. 1:7).
c. *Ask the Holy Spirit for power to be different* (Luke 11:13; Gal. 5:16, 22, 23).
d. *Move out in obedience to the Word of God, and make the necessary changes* (Phil. 2:12, 13; James 1:19-24).

---

*Grateful acknowledgement again is given to Robert D. Smith, M.D.

SUPPLEMENTARY READING FOR UNIT 3

Christian Living in the Home, Jay Adams, chapter 7.
A Biblical View of the Sexes, Florence Brown, chapter 8.
The Christian Family, Larry Christenson, chapter 5.

The Family First, Kenneth Gangel, chapter 3.
The Christian Home in a Changing World, Gene Getz, chapter 3.
Reformation for the Family, ed. Errol Hulse, Henry E. Walter Limited, Foxton, chapter 2.
Discovering the Intimate Marriage, R. C. Sproul, chapter 3.
Marriage Is for Love, Richard L. Strauss, chapter 8.
Christ in the Home, Robert Taylor, Jr., chapters 5 and 6.

DISCUSSION AND STUDY QUESTIONS FOR UNIT 3
UNITY THROUGH ROLE FULFILLMENT—THE OTHER SIDE OF THE COIN

Role of the Husband
To be completed by husband and wife together.

A. Study Ephesians 5:22-33, and answer the following questions:
1. What two words in Ephesians 5:22-33 summarize the husband's responsibility to his wife? Compare verse 23 with verse 25.

_____

2. What example or model must the husband keep in mind as he exercises the headship over the wife? Compare Ephesians 5:23 and Ephesians 1:22. What does this mean as far as the wife's freedom, responsibilities, and initiative are concerned? Does Christ delegate responsibility to us? Allow us to make mistakes? To use abilities and exert initiative?

_____

_____

_____

3. For whose benefit is the headship of Christ always exercised? Compare Ephesians 1:22; 5:25-27. For whose benefit should the headship of the husband be exercised? Note Ephesians 5:28.

_____

_____

4. Consider the ways that Christ loved the church and then apply them to the way a husband should love his wife.

a. _____

b. _____

c. _____

d. _____

e. _____

f. _____

5. Make a list of your wife's needs. Are you fulfilling them?

a. _____

b. _____

c. _____

d. _____

e. _____

f. _____

g. _____

h. _____

B. The Bible uses the word "manager" to describe the husband's position in the home. Note I Timothy 3:4, 5 in the New American Standard Version. What does this suggest about the manner in which a husband treats his wife and children?

_____

_____

_____

C. What ways can the husband exercise loving leadership according to the following verses?

1. Ephesians 5:29 _____

2. I Timothy 5:8 _____

3. I Peter 3:7 _____

4. Ephesians 6:4 _____

5. Colossians 3:19 _____

6. Proverbs 22:6 _____

7. Ephesians 5:25-27 _____

8. I Corinthians 7:3, 4, 5 _____

D. Proverbs 31:10-31 indicates that a good husband gives his wife great responsibilities and uses her gifts to the full. What gifts or ability does your wife have that you do not have? What areas of responsibility will you delegate to her? Compare Proverbs 31:10-31; I Timothy 5:14; Titus 2:4, 5; Psalm 128:3. (Warning: Do not force her to take responsibilities for which she is not equipped.)

1. _____

2. _____

3. _____

4. _____

5. _____

6. _____

7. _____

E. Proverbs 31:28 says that a husband ought to praise and express appreciation to his wife. Make a list of things which you appreciate about your partner. Make a list of ways you can express appreciation to her. (Suggestion: Ask your wife to enumerate the things you appreciate about her. This may be an eye opener to you. If she does not know what you appreciate about her, it is because you have not been expressing your appreciation. Let Adam's example of verbalizing his appreciation of Eve challenge you. Read Genesis 2:23.)

Things you appreciate	*Ways you can express appreciation*
1. _____	1. _____
2. _____	2. _____
3. _____	3. _____
4. _____	4. _____
5. _____	5. _____
6. _____	6. _____
7. _____	7. _____
8. _____	8. _____
9. _____	9. _____
10. _____	10. _____
11. _____	11. _____
12. _____	12. _____

F. Contrast the Bible's concept of love with the world's concept. Look up the following verses and note what each indicates about true love.

1. Ephesians 5:25 _____

2. John 3:16 _____

3. Galatians 2:20 _____

4. I John 3:16-18 _____

5. Romans 13:8-10 _____

6. Matthew 6:24 _____

7. Titus 2:3-5 _____

8. John 13:34 _____

9. Matthew 22:37-39 _____

10. Ephesians 5:2 _____

11. Luke 6:27-35 _____

12. Ephesians 4:2 _____

13. Romans 14:15 _____

14. I Peter 4:8 _____

15. Galatians 5:13 _____

16. Luke 10:25-37 _____

17. I Corinthians 8:1 _____

18. Proverbs 17:17 _____

19. Galatians 6:2 _____

G. I Corinthians 13:4-7 gives us the Bible's definition of love. These verses tell us that love consists of many elements—negative and positive. Consider the elements of love. Give an illustration of how each will be applied in your marriage. Be specific.
1. Suffers long—endures offenses, is not hasty, waits for the Lord to right all wrong.

   I will love my mate by _____

   _____

2. Is kind—not inconsiderate, seeks to help, is constructive, blesses when cursed, helps when hurt, demonstrates tenderness.

   I will love my mate by _____

   _____

41

3. Is not envious, but content—is not jealous of another person's success or competitive.

   I will love my mate by _____.

   _____

4. Is not arrogant, but humble—is not haughty, but lowly and gracious.

   I will love my mate by _____

   _____

5. Is not boastful, but reserved—does not show off, try to impress, want to be the center of attraction.

   I will love my mate by _____

   _____

6. Is not rude, but courteous.

   I will love my mate by _____

   _____

7. Is not selfish, but self-forgetful.

   I will love my mate by _____

   _____

8. Is not irritable, but good tempered.

   I will love my mate by _____

   _____

9. Is not vindictive or wrathful, but generous.

   I will love my mate by _____

   _____

10. Does not delight in bringing another person's sins to light, but will rejoice when another person obeys the truth.

I will love my mate by _____

_____

11. Is not rebellious, but brave, conceals rather than exposes another person's wrongdoing to others.

I will love my mate by _____

_____

12. Is not suspicious, but trustful, not cynical, makes every allowance, looks for an explanation that will show the best in others.

I will love my mate by _____

_____

13. Is not despondent, but hopeful, does not give up because it has been deceived or denied.

I will love my mate by _____

_____

14. Is not conquerable, but invincible—can outlast any trial, reproof, and problem.

I will love my mate by _____

_____

H. Make a list of any other ways not already mentioned by which a husband might love his wife.

1. _____

2. _____

3. _____

4. _____

5. _____

6. _____

7. _____

8. _____

9. _____

10. _____

11. _____

12. _____

13. _____

14. _____

15. _____

I. Discuss your personal habits that annoy your wife. Begin to work on correcting them unless to do so would contradict the Bible.

1. _____

2. _____

3. _____

4. _____

5. _____

6. _____

7. _____

8. _____

J. Discuss how you can be the head of your home, providing loving leadership without making your wife feel inferior or squelching her initiative and creativity.

1. _____

2. _____

3. _____

4. _____

5. _____

6. _____

7. _____

8. _____

K. What could you do to strengthen your marriage relationship?

1. _____

2. _____

3. _____

4. _____

5. _____

6. _____

7. _____

8. _____

9. _____

10. _____

Unity Developed Through Good Communication

Deep oneness can be achieved only where good communication exists. In this unit the necessity of good communication and principles leading to good communication are presented. Some practical suggestions, supplementary reading, study questions, and exercises for developing and maintaining good communication are included.

A. *No two people can effectively walk together, work together, or live together without a good communications system.*

1. Scripture asks, "Can two walk together except they be agreed" (Amos 3:3)? Wherever you find two people who are continuously and harmoniously walking together, striving toward the same goals, conducting their lives according to the same standards, giving mutual assistance, enjoying sweet fellowship with one another, you can be sure that they are in agreement.

2. And if they are in agreement, you can be sure that they have learned to communicate with one another. Continuous, progressive harmony and agreement are impossible without good communication. Good interpersonal relationships require good communication.

B. *Certainly, apart from our relationship to Himself, God intends the marriage relationship to be the closest of all interpersonal relationships.*

1. Concerning this relationship God said, "For this cause shall a man leave his father and mother and cleave to his wife, and the two shall become one flesh" (Gen. 2:24).

2. But can two people become one flesh without a good communication system? Absolutely not! To a large extent, a married couple's experience of genuine oneness will be determined by the health of their communication system. Nothing, except their union, communion, and communication with God in and through Jesus Christ, is more important to the development of genuine oneness.

   a. In his book, *Christian Living in the Home,* Jay Adams asserts that *communication comes first.* According to him Christian communication is "the basic skill needed to establish and maintain sound relationships. A sound husband and wife relationship is impossible apart from good communication" (pp. 27, 28).

   b. Along the same line, Dwight Hervey Small declares in his book, *After You've Said I Do,* that "the heart of marriage is its communications system. . . . It can be said that the success and

46

happiness of any married pair is measurable in terms of the deepening dialogue which characterizes their union" (p. 11).

    c. *Wherever you find marital failure, you will find a breakdown in real communication. Wherever you find marital success, you will find a good communication system.*

   3. This being the case, an examination of the biblical principles or requirements involved in good communications is essential to the development of genuine oneness.

I. *Surely, one of the basic requirements of good communications is mutual openness or honesty* (Eph. 4:25; I John 1:7-10).

   A. When Paul wrote the second epistle to the Corinthians, there was a problem in his relationship to them.

      1. Apparently, some members of the church had been spreading rumors about Paul. They suggested that Paul was a "con man" who could not be trusted (II Cor. 1:13-24; 2:17; 4:1, 2). They suggested that Paul did not really care about them at all. These accusers, of course, had never confronted Paul with these charges. Instead, when Paul had been there, they probably had pretended that everything was "sweetness and light" between them. Now, however, when he was not around, they sowed their seeds of character assassination and innuendo freely.

      2. Well, somehow Paul heard about what was happening. So he wrote to them to correct the matter and restore his good relations with them.

         a. On the one hand, he denied the validity of the charges. He said, "Our mouth is open to you, Corinthians—we are hiding nothing, keeping nothing back, and our heart is expanded wide. There is no lack of room for you in our hearts. . . . We have wronged no one; we have betrayed or corrupted no one; we have cheated or taken advantage of no one. . . . you are nested in our hearts" (II Cor. 6:11, 12; 7:2, 3).

         b. On the other hand, he held the Corinthians culpable. He says, "You lack room in your own affections for us. . . . I speak as to children—open wide your hearts also to us. . . . Do open your hearts to us again—enlarge them to take us in" (II Cor. 6:1, 12; 7:2, 3).

         c. Apparently, the Corinthians had shut up their hearts to Paul. In the context, this means that their affection for Paul had diminished and that they had not been open and honest with him. In effect, Paul is saying, "We are hiding, keeping nothing back. We have been open and honest with you. But you are the ones that have been holding back. You have been less than open and honest with us." And the result of this holding back

was a breakdown in the relationship between them.
B. *Openness and honesty of communication are essential to good relationships.*
   1. Scripture indicates that the truth about God is known only by revelation (Matt. 11:25; 16:17; I Cor. 2:6-15). If God had not given us the Scriptures; if God does not illuminate our minds to understand the Scriptures; if God does not communicate with us, we can never really know Him or have a close relationship with Him.
   2. *Similarly, Scripture indicates that if we are going really to know one another, we must open up and reveal ourselves to each other.*
      a. "For who among men knows the thoughts of a man except the spirit of a man, which is in him" (I Cor. 2:11)?
      b. "For as he thinks in his heart, so is he" (Prov. 23:7).
      c. I cannot really know my wife; she cannot really know me, unless we are open and honest with one another.
         1) She may think she knows me; I may think I know her by observation, and to some degree maybe we do. But we cannot really know each other or relate to one another in depth until we open wide our hearts.
         2) Not what my wife may pretend to be, not what I think my wife is, not what others think my wife is, but what she thinks in her heart, that she is. And unless I am relating to what she is in her heart, I am relating to a phantom, an image, a mirage, and not the real person.
      d. Often in marriage counseling, a counselor will hear words such as these: "I did not know you felt that way," or "I did not know that what I was doing was annoying you," or "I did not know that such and such a thing was important to you," or "I did not know you wanted me to do that." For example, a couple who have been married for many years knows that something is missing in their relationship. They cannot seem to relate to one another, and they do not know what is wrong. He gets ticked off at the smallest thing, and she does the same. They are Christians, and they know it is not right. It is not good for their testimony. Nor is it good for their children. So, finally, they swallow their pride and approach their pastor about their problem. He probes a bit and then asks the wife to describe what it is about her husband that annoys her. She gulps, screws up her courage and begins to share some little things that have been bothering her for years. When she is finished, her husband responds by saying, "Honey, why didn't you tell me about these things before? I did not know that this is what was bothering you. I thought it was. . . ." At this point the pastor, know-

48

ing that there are two sides to every story, turns to the husband and asks him to describe what has been annoying him. The husband opens up and shares what has been annoying him, to which the wife replies, "That's what has been bothering you? I didn't know. Why didn't you talk to me about these things?"

    e. In this real life illustration, the husband and wife could not really relate to one another because they did not know one another. And they did not know one another because they were holding back, refusing to open up and allow themselves to be known. Probably they began to do this for what they thought were good reasons—they did not want to stir up a fuss; they did not want to hurt the other person; it was such a small thing; the Bible says that we are to turn the other cheek; the other person may get angry or reject me. In the end, when covering up what they really thought and refusing to discuss disagreements or differences of opinion had become a way of life, the little things had begun to pile up. Unresolved little issues had been blown out of proportion, and an accumulation of little issues had formed a large, invisible barrier between them.

3. Scripture enjoins us to "be angry and sin not; do not ever let your wrath—your exasperation—last until the sun goes down. Leave no such room or foothold for the devil—give no opportunity to him" (Eph. 4:26, 27—Amplified Version). Applied to the marriage relationship, this means that the sources of irritation between the husband and wife must be dealt with immediately and conclusively.

    a. On the one hand, there are times when it is right to deal with the problem by really covering, disregarding, forgiving, or forgetting the fault or annoyance of the other person (I Pet. 4:8; Prov. 10:12; I Cor. 13:5, 7).

    b. If, however, this cannot or should not be done (because it would bring reproach on Christ or harm to each other) the issue must be lovingly and boldly faced, discussed, and, if possible, resolved.

    c. It is patently clear then that close, genuine relationships can thrive only in the soil of openness and honesty. *When I say this, I am not suggesting that a married couple must "let it all hang out."* Scripture warns us that there are some things of which it is a shame to think or speak (Eph. 4:29; 5:3, 4; Matt. 5:27, 28; Phil. 4:8).

2. Several biblical principles must guide us, even with our married partners, in the exercise of openness and honesty. I state those principles in the form of questions and hope that we will memorize and use them to guide all our communication efforts.

a. Is it really *true?* Do I really have the facts (Eph. 4:29; Prov. 18:13)?
b. Is what I would like to say *profitable?* Will it help or hurt? Be constructive or destructive (Prov. 20:15; Eph. 4:29; Rom. 15:1-3)?
c. Is this the *proper time* for me to say it, or would it be better for me to wait (Prov. 15:23, 28; 25:11, 12)?
d. Is my *attitude* right (Eph. 4:15, 32; I Cor. 16:14; Titus 3:1, 2)?
e. Are the *words* that I will use the best possible way of saying it (Prov. 12:25; 15:1, 23; 16:23; Eccles. 12:10)?
f. Have I *prayed* about this matter, and am I trusting God to help me (Prov. 3:5, 6; Col. 4:2-6; Ps. 19:14)?

3. As I have already stated, no couple can really become one without openness and honesty in communication. At the same time, *it must be the right kind of openness and honesty.* Otherwise, it will destroy rather than enhance good relations. These six questions can provide guidelines for the exercise of proper openness in communications.

II. From what has just been said, it becomes evident that *self-control is a requirement for good communication.*

A. Sometimes I have heard people joke about having a "short fuse."
1. Or they say defensively, "I get angry quickly, but I get over it right away."
2. Or after they have just engaged in a fantastic display of fireworks, "I believe in calling a spade a spade. I believe in speaking my mind, but I do not really mean anything by it. You can ask anyone; I do not hold grudges."

B. Well, I assure you that *having a "short fuse" is not a joking matter.*
1. Dr. James Kennedy has said, "I have noticed over the years in talking with people who make that statement (I believe in calling a spade a spade) that it is always the other people's spades they are talking about. They may speak the truth, but they are about as loving as a bucketfull of hydrochloric acid." (Published sermon entitled "Communication in the Home.")
2. Living with someone who has a "short fuse" is not a very pleasant experience.
a. Who enjoys living at the foot of an active volcano? Who enjoys having hot lava poured out over him on a regular basis? At first it may be rather exciting, but after a while it becomes somewhat frightening.
b. Who enjoys living on top of a time bomb that goes off at frequent intervals?
c. And who enjoys being the object of frequent expressions of

50

bitterness, resentment, anger, wrath, and clamor? Who wants to be yelled at and screamed at? Who delights in living with a person who lacks control over his violent temper? Who feels free to communicate openly with someone who easily becomes irritated and touchy and resentful and vindictive?

C. The old saw, "sticks and stones may break my bones, but words can never hurt me," is emphatically untrue.

1. *The Bible has a lot to say about the destructive power of wrong speech.*

   a. Scripture asserts that our words can be as dangerous and painful and destructive as "the piercing of a sword" or as a cup of poison or as the burning of a fire (Prov. 12:18; 16:27; James 3:5-8).

   b. It further states that our words can be like a large sledge hammer or sharp arrow, bringing ruin, devastation, destruction, and death.

2. Because of a lack of self control, many a wound has been inflicted, many a painful blow has been struck, many a marriage has been poisoned or sabotaged.

   a. Hateful, violent, vindictive, hasty, careless, bitter, cutting words have been hurled at the other person with great velocity and frequency, leaving the other person battered, beaten, weary, and hopeless.

   b. The result? Lines of communication are shut down, and the marriage relationship deteriorates. John and Mary's marriage was really in a serious condition. Divorce had been contemplated many times, and Mary was again convinced that this was the only solution. As they sat in the counselor's office, animosity was so thick you could almost cut it with a knife. Mary sat there looking dejected and thoroughly defeated. She hung her head and acted like a scared rabbit. Her eyes flitted from one place to another, unwilling to look anyone in the eye. Not very far into the counseling session it became evident that John had a violent temper over which he exerted no control. His normal way of reacting to conflict of opinion, criticism, or difficulty of any kind was to stand up, pace back and forth, and speak in a very irritated, dogmatic, defensive, and loud tone of voice. This had become a pattern, a habit for him. And it had had a devastating effect upon his wife's attitude toward herself and life, and also upon his own relationship to her. To be sure, her response to his violent temper was wrong, but he had provided the environment in which these deadly weeds had grown. His lack of self-control over his emotions, his cutting, demeaning,

51

condemning, critical, and boisterous words had created an atmosphere in which significant and meaningful communication had died. Their marriage serves as a tragic illustration of the fact that self-control of one's words and emotions is a requirement for good communication.

D. *There are, however, two other forms of self control which are equally important to good communication.*

   1. *One is the ability to control yourself when you are tempted to retreat into silence or go off and have a good pout.*

      a. Perhaps there are times when "silence is golden." But if that is your usual way of responding to opposition, conflict, honest differences of opinion, criticism, or disagreement, you will never develop a close relationship with anyone.

      b. One woman prided herself on the fact that she had never yelled at her husband. Nor had she ever verbally disagreed with him. Instead, when conflict arose, she would become silent. When her husband became increasingly cool toward her with less and less to say, she could not understand it. She had always been such a submissive wife, or, at least, so she thought.

      c. What this woman failed to realize was that her husband did not want a silent partner for a wife. He wanted a companion, a helper, someone to whom he could talk; someone with whom he could intelligently discuss issues; someone to stimulate and quietly challenge and clarify his thinking by presenting another point of view. But his wife never did that. She just became silent.

      d. I am not saying that a woman should be argumentative, loud, and boisterous. She is to be of a meek and quiet spirit (I Pet. 3:3, 4). Yet Scripture says of God's ideal wife, "She opens her mouth with wisdom, and the teaching of kindness is on her tongue" (Prov. 31:26).

      e. The temptation to respond continuously to disagreement with silence must then be avoided if good communication is to be maintained. Instead, self-control must be exercised, issues must be faced, disagreements and conflicts must be calmly, respectfully, and fully discussed.

   2. *One other important aspect of self-control that must be mentioned is the control of "crocodile tears" or "manipulative tears."*

      a. I asked a pastor friend of mine the question, "What hinders good communication between you and your wife?" Immediately he responded by saying, "The one thing that really turns me off is when my wife turns on the tears. When she does that, I do not know what to do. I do not know what to say. I do not know how to handle it. I just give up. The lines of communication become jammed."

    b. Now I do not believe this man was talking about tears of sympathy or tears of concern or tears of sorrow over sin. I think he was referring to tears of self pity, to crocodile tears, to manipulative tears, to tears that are shed because the other person does not want to face the issues or is hurt because someone disagreed or disapproved.

    c. When hurts or disapproval or conflict come, it is easy for some of us to give way to tears. This then becomes our natural, habitual response to hard situations. We must, however, pray for the help of the Holy Spirit to exercise control and change our response, because manipulative or crocodile tears will clog the circuits of good marital communication.

III. *Implied in the communication principles that have already been stated, but requiring further emphasis and amplification, is the need for a charitable, forbearing, accepting spirit.*

    A. When we talk about controlling our temper or words or tears, we are talking about controlling things that are hindrances or barriers to good communication.

        1. Significantly, when Paul discusses the matter of Christian interpersonal relationships in Ephesians he says, "Let no foul or polluting language, nor evil word, nor unwholesome or worthless talk ever come out of your mouth. . . . Let all bitterness and indignation and wrath (passion, rage, bad temper) and resentment (anger, animosity) and quarreling (brawling, clamor, contention) and slander (evil speaking, abusive or blasphemous language) be banished from you with all malice (spite, ill will or baseness of any kind)" (Eph. 4:29, 31—Amplified Version).

        2. *These reactions must be controlled, they must be banished from our lives if genuine oneness is to be experienced in the marriage relationship.*

    B. *But controlling these negative reactions is not enough.*

        1. In the words of Paul, we must not only put off certain things; we must also put on certain things.

        2. True, we must stop reacting in an improper way, but we also must begin acting in a biblical way.

        3. We must replace sinful practices with holy, righteous practices.

    C. In reference to good communication, *this means that our judgmental, critical, demanding, officious, demeaning, bitter spirit must be replaced with a charitable, encouraging, forbearing, accepting spirit.*

        1. Ephesians 4:2 admonishes us to "live as becomes us—with complete lowliness of mind and meekness (unselfishness, gentleness,

mildness) with patience, *bearing with one another and making allowances,* because you love one another."

2. Verse 29 of the same chapter commands us to use "only such speech as is good and beneficial to the spiritual progress of others, *as is fitting to the need and occasion,* that it may be a blessing and give grace to those who hear it."

3. Verse 32 instructs us to *"become useful and helpful and kind to one another,* tenderhearted (compassionate, understanding, lovinghearted), *forgiving one another* (readily and freely), as God in Christ forgave you."

D. *Within a context where the attitudes and actions described by Paul exist, good communication is the inevitable result.*

1. It is not hard for a wife to be open and honest with a husband who is lowly in mind and meek and patient. It is not hard for a woman to communicate freely with her husband when she knows that he will bear with her and make allowances for her rather than condemn and demean her.

2. Likewise, the wife who makes it a practice to use only such speech as is good and beneficial and fitting to the need and occasion; the wife who readily and freely forgives and seeks to be helpful and kind to her husband will make it very easy for her husband to open up and share his life with her. In such a non-threatening, understanding atmosphere the husband has no reason for pretense or putting on a false front or practicing deceit or hiding his fears, frustrations, faults, and anxieties. He knows he is accepted as he is and for what he is. He knows his wife is for him and will help him rather than judge and condemn him.

E. *To say that good communication requires a charitable, forbearing spirit does not mean that the husband and wife must condone error or evil.*

1. Scripture warns against compromise and rebukes those who call "evil good."

a. There will be times when a husband must disagree with his wife and point out her error or sin (Eph. 5:25-27).

b. There will be times when a wife must do the same to her husband. Sapphira was wrong for going along with Ananias in his wicked scheme. She should have lovingly admonished him and refused to cooperate in sin (Acts 5:1-11).

2. Certainly Paul is not encouraging us to condone sin or cooperate in sin when he tells us to bear with and make allowances for one another. Rather, he is encouraging an attitude of complete commitment, loyalty, fidelity, sensitivity, unselfishness to the other person. What he is encouraging is a love for the other person that "bears all things, believes all things, hopes all things, endures all

54

things"; a love which cannot be quenched; a love which *really* has the other person's best interests at heart.

IV. *Of all the principles involved in effective communication, none is more important than good listening.*

   A. *Good communication is a two-way street involving free, open conversation and careful, attentive listening.* It involves both the sending and receiving of a message. Without both, good communication is impossible.

   1. Have you ever had the experience of talking to someone when you get the impression he is not really listening to you at all? While you are talking his eyes are moving all over the place or else he is yawning or looking at you with a blank stare.

      a. Well, that type of thing does not encourage good communication.

      b. Instead, you get the idea that what you are saying is not interesting or important. You then lose your desire to talk to that person or, even worse, you lose confidence in yourself as a conversationalist. Of this you can be sure, poor listening stifles effective communication.

   2. On the other hand, good listening promotes effective communication.

      a. Ask any preacher what happens to him when people gladly receive the Word which he is preaching.

      b. Watch what happens when a mother gives her full attention to what a child has to say to her.

      c. Scripture says, "Counsel in the heart of a man is like water in a deep well, but a man of understanding will draw it out" (Prov. 20:5). Because of various opportunities and experiences, every man has some insights and wisdom to share, but some men seem to have difficulty sharing those insights. They have water, but it seems to be so deep within them that it cannot be reached. How do you prime the pump? You will never get the water out as long as you talk on and on about yourself, your ideas, your plans, your activities, your insights. You will get it out when you are willing to stop talking and really listen. Perhaps you will have to prime the pump by asking the right kind of questions about things in which they are interested and knowledgeable. But if you ask the right questions and prove that you really are interested in what they have to say, many quiet people will suddenly become great talkers. Good listening is to communication what a magnet is to iron or a siphon is to a gas tank. It has drawing power. It gets the conversation flowing.

   B. *To gain additional insight into the communication process, I want to share several factors about good listening.*

1. *Good listening involves letting the other person speak without interruption.*
   a. Proverbs 18:13 says that it is folly and shame to answer a matter before you hear it.
   b. By this standard many husbands and wives are fools and ought to be ashamed, for they constantly interrupt one another when they are talking. Here is a woman who starts to tell a story. She says, "Last week we went for a drive on Route 352 and. . . ." "No dear," her husband interrupts, "it was not Route 352. It was Route 252." "Oh yes, you're right. Well anyway, we were traveling down Route 252 at about 45 miles. . . ." "I hate to interrupt you again," says the husband, "but we were not going 45 miles an hour. We were going 47½ miles an hour. I distinctly remember looking at the speedometer, and it did read 47½ miles an hour." Well, the wife makes several other attempts and is interrupted repeatedly. Finally, she gives up and says, "You tell the story."
   c. This, of course, is an exaggerated illustration, but it is the type of thing that often happens in conversations where people either interrupt to make corrections or additions or to add emphasis to what has been said. And of this you can be sure—when this happens consistently, effective communication grinds to a standstill.
2. *Good listening involves giving the other person your undivided attention* (Prov. 18:13; James 1:19).
   a. Whenever possible you should stop whatever you are doing and concentrate on what the other person is saying. If you are fixing the automobile, pause and give your wife your full attention. If you are washing the dishes, stop what you are doing and direct all of your faculties toward your husband. Sometimes this may not be feasible, but do it whenever you can. If you cannot pause immediately, explain that you are in the midst of something and cannot stop entirely but that you will be willing to do so as soon as possible. Communicate the impression that your relationship to one another is more important than anyone or anything else.
   b. Another aspect involved in giving the other person your full attention is guarding against the temptation to tune the other person out either because you really do not want to hear what he is saying or because you are thinking about the good answer you are going to give. Perhaps you try to give the impression you are interested in what the other person is saying. In reality you are not. What you are really interested in is how you are

going to defend yourself, display your wisdom, crack a good joke, or straighten the other person out. If you do this frequently with your mate, she will sense it. And the message she will receive is, "He really does not care about my ideas. He is not interested in what I have to say."

3. *Good listening involves making sure you really understand what the other person is saying or thinking.*

   a. In his book, *Discovering the Intimate Marriage,* R. C. Sproul tells about a time when he gave a lecture and then conducted a discussion on the lecture. One person asked him a question about a word in his lecture. He said he could not remember using the word. Someone else suggested that he had used a completely different word. Immediately the group became divided—some affirming that he had used the one word and the others declaring that he had used the other. To settle the dispute, the tape of the lecture was played. To the surprise of everyone, the tape revealed that he had used neither word (pp. 15, 16).

   b. Both groups thought they knew what he had said. Both thought they understood him, but both were wrong. Surely this illustration points out the importance of making sure that we really hear the other person and understand what he meant by what he said. What we think he said or meant is not the issue. What he did say and mean is.

   c. People often heard the words of Jesus and thought that He meant something He never meant. (Compare John 2:19; 6:51; Mark 8:15, 16.) Jesus Christ was history's clearest and best communicator. Yet men misunderstood Him and misquoted Him.

   d. Let that then be a warning to us as we listen to others. What we think they mean and what they do mean may sometimes be two different things. Fairness demands that before we put the worst possible interpretation on what someone says, we ought to do some checking. We ought to ask some questions. Perhaps if we do not like what someone has said, we ought to assume that we have misinterpreted him. For example, if a husband says to his wife, "I want you to know I am praying for you," she should not respond by saying, "I wonder what he thinks is wrong with me now. He is never satisfied. He is always trying to change me." Rather she should assume, "He must really be concerned about me. He knows about my trials and fears and wants God to strengthen me. That man really loves me." Or if a wife says to her husband, "I thought you would never

57

come home," it would be wrong for him to think, "There she goes complaining again. I cannot do anything right. She wants to run my life." Instead, unless he has proof to the contrary, he should assume she means, "I really missed you. I love you so much I can hardly wait for you to return."

    e.   *Inherent in the whole communication-listening dynamic is the necessity to try to see things from the other person's point of view.* To see things from the other person's perspective may require repeating what he has said back to him until he is satisfied that you do understand. Or it may involve asking him kindly to say it in a different or amplified way until you are sure you understand.

V. Conclusion.

    A.   As has already been stated, effective communication involves good listening as well as good speaking. You cannot have one without the other. May God help us then to apply all of these principles so that we will become better communicators.

    B.   Remember God's purpose for marriage involves two people becoming one flesh (Gen. 2:24). God wants the husband and wife to be totally and completely one. He wants them to have a shared life.

       1.   This is the goal toward which we should strive. It is a goal which by the power of the Holy Spirit can be to some extent realized here and now provided:

           a.   The two of you have repented of your sins and are trusting in Jesus Christ.

           b.   The two of you have accepted God's revealed will concerning your respective roles and are attempting to fulfill them.

           c.   The two of you are seeking to develop and maintain an ever-deepening and expanding communications system.

       2.   I urge you, then, to review the material on communications, noting where you are weak.

           a.   Ask God to help you make the changes that are necessary. Trust Him to do it.

           b.   Begin seriously to implement and apply the biblical principles enunciated in this manual (Phil. 2:12, 13).

       3.   In the marriage relationship, communication may be termed survival. It is not optional but vital. It is the life stream, the nerve, the heart beat. Where it is lacking, the marriage relationship deteriorates and dies. Where it is healthy, the marriage relationship flourishes, and the two become one.

TWELVE PRACTICAL SUGGESTIONS FOR DEVELOPING AND MAINTAINING GOOD MARITAL COMMUNICATIONS

1. When there are problems, each must be willing to admit that he/she is part of the problem. (Gen. 8:8-19; Prov. 20:6)
2. Each person must be willing to change. (John 5:6; Matt. 5:23-26)
3. Avoid the use of emotionally charged words. "You don't really love me." "You *always* do. . . ." "You *never* do anything right." "I don't care."
4. Be responsible for your own emotions, words, actions, and reactions. Don't blame them on the other person. You got angry, lashed out, became depressed, etc. (Gal. 6:5; James 1:13-15)
5. Refrain from having reruns on old arguments. (Eph. 4:26)
6. Deal with one problem at a time. Solve one problem and then move on to the next. (Matt. 6:34 principle)
7. Deal in the present and not in the past. Hang a "no fishing" sign over the past unless it will help you to solve your present problems. (Phil. 3:12-14; Jer. 31:34; Isa. 43:25)
8. Major on the positive instead of majoring on the negative. (Phil. 4:8)
9. Learn to communicate in non-verbal ways. (Matt. 8:1, 2, 14, 15; Ps. 32:8)
10. Express your thoughts and concerns to each other. Relate your activities. Listen, understand, and respond to the meaning behind what a person is saying. When he flies off the handle at you, he may be saying, "I've had a terrible day at the job. Nobody respects me." When he says, "You don't love me," he may be really saying, "I desperately need some affection. I'm starved for love." (Example of Jesus in John 1:45-47; Mark 5:1-15; John 11:20-35)
11. Practice the golden rule—Matthew 7:12. What would you like your mate to do to you? Would you like your mate to: Tell you the truth? Ask your opinion? Help in time of need? Be natural around you? Thank you for your help or services? Well, then do the same for him.
12. Practice the principle laid down in Luke 6:35. "Do good—do that which will help others; and lend expecting and hoping for nothing in return."

SUPPLEMENTARY READING FOR UNIT 4

Christian Living in the Home, Jay Adams, chapter 3.
Building a Christian Home, Henry Brandt and Homer Dowdy, Scripture Press, Wheaton, 1960, chapter 5.
Say It With Love, Howard G. Hendricks, Victor Books, Wheaton, 1974, chapter 8.
The Christian Home, Shirley Rice, lesson 7.
After You've Said I Do, Dwight Small, Revell, Old Tappan, 1968, whole book.
Discovering the Intimate Marriage, R. C. Sproul, chapters 1 and 2.

Marriage Is for Love, Richard L. Strauss, chapters 10 and 11.
Communication: Key to Your Marriage, H. Norman Wright, Regal Publications, Glendale, 1974, chapters 4 to 9.

DISCUSSION AND STUDY QUESTIONS FOR UNIT 4
UNITY THROUGH EFFECTIVE COMMUNICATION

To be completed together by husband and wife.

A worksheet designed to help you evaluate your present success
as a communicator and to discover how to improve.

A. Consider and discuss what happens when people do not communicate effectively.
   1. Issues remain unclarified (Prov. 18:17).
   2. Wrong ideas are uncorrected.
   3. Conflicts and misunderstandings are unresolved (Matt. 5:23-26).
   4. Confusion and disorder occur (I Cor. 14:33, 40).
   5. Wise decision-making is thwarted (Prov. 18:13).
   6. The development of deep unity and intimacy is hindered (Amos 3:3).
   7. Boredom, discontentment, and frustration develop.
   8. Interpersonal problems pile up and barriers become higher and wider.
   9. Temptation to look for someone more exciting occurs.
   10. We do not really get to know each other.
   11. We do not receive spiritual help from each other.
B. Consider and discuss various methods of communication. Verbal communication is only one aspect of communication.
   1. Visually (wink, closed eyes, etc.).
   2. Verbally (harsh voice, soft voice, etc., what you say or do not say and how you say it).
   3. By notes or letters.
   4. By smiles or frowns (facial expressions).
   5. With your body (hands, feet, etc.).
   6. By your presence or absence.
   7. By a touch or a pat or a hug.
   8. By helping.
   9. By a gift.
   10. By the use of your talents or gifts.
   11. By willingness or unwillingness to share.
   12. By listening or not listening.
C. Discuss different levels of communication—how have you and can you com-

municate on these levels? Give at least one instance, if you can, of how the
two of you have communicated on each of these levels. Circle the levels where
you have the greatest difficulty in communication.
1. Cliché level.
2. Casual conversation.
3. Sharing information or facts.
4. Supportive or encouraging or motivating.
5. Sharing ideas, opinions, feelings, emotions, or judgments.
6. Planning or decision-making.
7. Corrective, instructive, reproving, or challenging.
8. Disagreements or controversial issues.
D. Discuss what has hindered your communication in the past. Think of issues
or times when you have not communicated well and analyze what happened.

1. _____

2. _____

3. _____

4. _____

5. _____

6. _____

7. _____

8. _____

9. _____

10. _____

E. Make a list of all your unresolved conflicts or disagreements. Begin to work
on them one by one. Pray together about these problems. Find biblical so-
lutions.

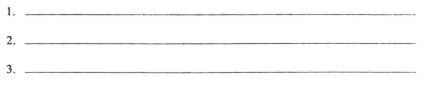

1. _____

2. _____

3. _____

4. _____

5. _____

6. _____

7. _____

8. _____

9. _____

10. _____

F. Have each person express how or what he/she would like the other person to tell him about. Make a list.

1. _____

2. _____

3. _____

4. _____

5. _____

G. Communicate every day with your spouse. When? Make this a priority matter.

H. Make a list of helps to good communication. Look up the following verses.

1. Ephesians 4:15, 25 _____

2. Ephesians 4:29 _____

3. Ephesians 4:26, 27 _____

4. Ephesians 4:32 _____

5. Psalm 141:3 _____

6. Isaiah 50:4 _____

7. Ecclesiastes 12:10 _____

8. Proverbs 12:25 _____

9. Proverbs 15:2 _____

10. Proverbs 15:28 _____

11. Proverbs 15:1 _____

12. Proverbs 15:23 _____

13. Proverbs 17:14 _____

14. Proverbs 18:23 _____

15. Proverbs 20:5 _____

16. Proverbs 20:15 _____

17. Proverbs 25:9 _____

18. Proverbs 25:11, 12 _____

19. Proverbs 25:15 _____

20. Proverbs 29:11 _____

21. Proverbs 31:26 _____

22. Galatians 5:13 _____

23. Romans 13:7, 8 _____

24. Proverbs 5:18, 19 _____

25. Ephesians 5:33 & I Peter 3:1-7 _____

I. Make a list of things that are circuit jammers (hindrances to good communication).

1. Ephesians 4:25 _____

2. Ephesians 4:29 _____

3. Ephesians 4:31 _____

4. Colossians 3:8 _____

5. Colossians 3:9 _____

6. Proverbs 11:12 _____

7. Proverbs 11:13 _____

8. Proverbs 12:16 _____

9. Proverbs 12:18 _____

10. Proverbs 15:1 _____

11. Proverbs 15:5 _____

12. Proverbs 16:27 _____

13. Proverbs 17:9 _____

14. Proverbs 18:2 _____

15. Proverbs 18:6 _____

16. Proverbs 18:8 _____

17. Proverbs 18:13 _____

18. Proverbs 18:17 _____

19. Proverbs 18:23 _____

20. Proverbs 19:1 _____

21. Proverbs 19:5 _____

22. Proverbs 20:25 _____

23. Proverbs 20:19 _____

24. Proverbs 25:24 _____

25. Proverbs 26:18, 19 _____

26. Proverbs 26:20, 21 _____

27. Proverbs 26:22 _____

28. Proverbs 27:2 _____

29. Proverbs 29:20 _____

J. Examine your effectiveness as a communicator.
   1. Consider what you have discovered about hindrances to good communications and note what circuit jammers need to be eliminated. (Ask your mate honestly to evaluate you.)

   a. _____

   b. _____

   c. _____

   d. _____

   e. _____

   f. _____

   g. _____

   h. _____

   2. What helps need to be added or strengthened? (Ask your mate honestly to evaluate you.)

   a. _____

   b. _____

   c. _____

   d. _____

   e. _____

f. _____

g. _____

h. _____

K. Keep a record of the times when you expressed concern and appreciation for the ideas, desires, interests, feelings, and actions of your mate this week. Plan to do this often.

1. _____

2. _____

3. _____

4. _____

5. _____

6. _____

7. _____

8. _____

L. List several occasions when you have admitted to your mate that you were wrong and asked for forgiveness. Describe the circumstances. This will promote good communication.

1. _____

2. _____

3. _____

4. _____

M. Discover and list the following items about your mate. Talk to him about these things. Become concerned about the things that concern him.
   1. Chief interests.
   2. Greatest fears.
   3. Greatest likes.

4. Greatest dislikes.
5. Greatest aspirations.
6. Greatest disappointments.
7. Greatest joys.

N. Make a list of what, when, and how you criticized your mate this week. Avoid all unnecessary criticism.

1. _____

2. _____

3. _____

4. _____

5. _____

O. Make a list of things you can do to please your mate (Phil. 2:3, 4). Put the list into practice. There are many ways of saying, "I care. I love you." Learn them. This will promote good communication.

1. _____

2. _____

3. _____

4. _____

5. _____

6. _____

7. _____

8. _____

9. _____

10. _____

P. Make a list of fun things you can do with your mate. Begin to put the list into practice. Build up a memory bank of commonalities and happy experiences. They become the grist for good communication.

1. _____

2. _____

3. _____

4. _____

5. _____

6. _____

7. _____

8. _____

9. _____

10. _____

Q. Evaluate the communication quotient of your marriage. On a scale of 1 to 10, where would you rate your communication with your spouse?

0 1 2 3 4 5 6 7 8 9 10

Very   Average   Excellent
Poor

Is your communication with your spouse improving or decreasing or remaining the same? Circle the arrow which indicates the direction your marital communication is going.

Decreasing   Staying   Improving
                The Same

Honestly take stock of what is happening, and then get to work because, in many respects, good communication is the heart throb, the key to a good marriage. And remember, until we get to heaven—there is always room for improvement.

DISCUSSION AND STUDY QUESTIONS FOR UNIT 4

MAINTAINING AND DEVELOPING UNITY IN MARRIAGE
BY CONTROLLING ANGER, BITTERNESS AND RESENTMESNT

To be completed together by husband and wife.

A. Describe the last three situations in which you became angry.

1. _____

_____

2. _____

_____

3. _____

_____

B. Discern and write down what the following verses have to say about the *wrong* way to handle anger.
1. Ephcsians 4:26, 27: Refuse to admit that you are angry, clam up, and pretend nothing is wrong. Make this way of dealing with anger a practice.
2. Proverbs 17:14: When you become angry, pick a fight as soon as you can. Be as nasty as you can.

3. Proverbs 29:11, 20 _____

_____

4 Matthew 5:21, 22 _____

_____

5. Ephesians 4:31 _____

_____

6. Proverbs 26:21 _____

_____

7. Proverbs 15:1 _____ _____

    _____

8. Colossians 3:8 _____

    _____

9. Romans 12:17, 19 _____

    _____

10. I Peter 3:9 _____

    _____

11. I Corinthians 13:5 _____

    _____

12. Philippians 4:8 _____

    _____

C. Discern and write down what the following verses have to say about the *right* way to handle anger.

  1. Romans 12:19-21: Never take your own revenge; turn the matter of punishment over to God; seek to help your enemy in specific ways.

  2. Ephesians 4:26: Acknowledge that you are angry, and seek to solve the problem immediately. Do not allow unresolved problems to pile up.

  3. Ephesians 4:29 _____

    _____

  4. Ephesians 4:32 _____

    _____

  5. Matthew 5:43, 44 _____

    _____

6. Proverbs 19:11 _____

_____

7. Proverbs 15:1 _____

_____

8. Proverbs 15:28 _____

_____

9. Proverbs 16:32 _____

_____

10. Proverbs 25:28 _____

_____

11. Proverbs 14:29 _____

_____

12. Proverbs 29:11 _____

_____

13. Psalm 37:1-11 _____

_____

14. I Peter 3:9 _____

_____

15. Galatians 5:16-23 _____

_____

16. Romans 8:28, 29 _____

_____

17. Matthew 5:1-12; I Thessalonians 5:18 _____

_____

18. Ephesians 5:20 _____

_____

19. I Corinthians 10:13 _____

_____

20. Genesis 50:20 _____

_____

21. James 4:6 _____

_____

22. I Corinthians 6:19, 20 _____

_____

23. Matthew 8:21-35 _____

_____

D. Examine your own life in the light of Matthew 5:1-12; Galatians 5:22, 23; and
II Peter 1:5-8, and list the qualities mentioned in these passages which are
most lacking in your life. Ask your mate for his evaluation.

1. _____

2. _____

3. _____

4. _____

5. _____

6. _____

7. _____

8. _____

9. _____

10. _____

11. _____

12. _____

E. Discuss how God may use your present irritations and annoyances to reveal your lack of these qualities and to develop them.

F. Consider and write out some of the benefits that your problems or irritations may bring to you.
   1. Isaiah 43:1-3: Communion and fellowship with God.
   2. I Corinthians 11:31, 32: Stimulates self examination.
   3. Psalm 119:71: New insight into Scripture.

   4. Romans 5:2-5 _____

   5. II Corinthians 1:3-6 _____

   6. Hebrews 12:5-11 _____

   7. II Corinthians 12:7-10 _____

   8. Matthew 5:10-12 _____

   9. I Peter 4:12-16 _____

   10. Psalm 119:67 _____

   11. Psalm 50:15 _____

   12. Philippians 3:10 _____

   13. James 1:2-5 _____

   14. I Peter 1:7 _____

G. Which of the following do you consider to be "your rights"?

1. Right to have and control personal belongings _____

2. Right to privacy _____

3. Right to have and express personal opinions _____

4. Right to earn and use money _____

5. Right to plan your own schedule _____

6. Right to be respected _____

7. Right to have and choose friends _____

8. Right to belong, be loved, be accepted _____

9. Right to be understood _____

10. Right to be supported _____

11. Right to make your own decisions _____

12. Right to determine your own future _____

13. Right to have good health _____

14. Right to have children _____

15. Right to be considered worthwhile and important _____

16. Right to be protected and cared for _____

17. Right to have the job you want _____

18. Right to a good education _____

19. Right to be appreciated _____

20. Right to travel _____

21. Right to have fun _____

22. Right to be a "beautiful person" _____

74

23. Right to be treated fairly _____

24. Right to be desired _____

25. Right to raise children your way _____

26. Right to security and safety _____

27. Right to fulfill hopes and aspirations _____

28. Right to be successful _____

29. Right to have others obey you _____

30. Right to have you own way _____

31. Right to be free of difficulties and problems_____

32. Others _____

H. Which of the aforementioned "rights" are you being denied by your mate?

1. _____

2. _____

3. _____

4. _____

5. _____

6. _____

7. _____

8. _____

9. _____

10. _____

I. Consciously recognize that if you are a Christian you, all you have, and are (your rights included) belong to God (I Cor. 6:19, 20; Rom. 12:1; Ps. 24:1). Acknowledge this and dedicate all that you are and have, including your "rights," to God. Trust Him to take care of His property. Cease to think in terms of "your rights," and concentrate on God's will and purpose and promises.

J. Whenever you are tempted to become sinfully angry, *write down:*
   1. What is happening?
   2. What qualities God may be trying to develop through this situation? (Thank Him for the benefits and opportunities this situation provides, and ask Him for His help.)
   3. What personal rights of yours do you think are being denied? (Turn yourself and your "rights" over to God.)
   4. What may you have done to promote the situation? (Confess your wrong attitudes, actions, or speech to God and the people involved, and ask forgiveness.)
   5. What does God want you to do, and how does He want you to act at this time? (Search the Scriptures, especially the passages mentioned under points C, D, E, and G; ask Him to help you to do what you should; depend upon Him to assist you and move out in obedience.)
   6. What is keeping you from doing the right thing when you are tempted to become sinfully angry? (Is it your ignorance? Lack of desire? Fear? etc. Seek help from your pastor or a Christian counselor if you do not know what to do.)

Unity Through Financial Agreement

Deep unity is often hindered because of differing views on money. In this unit biblical principles about finances are presented. Practical suggestions for the implementation of these principles are given. Suggested supplementary reading, study questions, and action plans are included. As husbands and wives study and apply the content of this unit, financial disagreements can be overcome and unity will be promoted.

A. Genesis 2:24 indicates that God's purpose for marriage is that two people should become one.
   1. Scripturally speaking, *marriage is a total commitment and a total sharing of your total person with another person until death.*
   2. *Included in the total sharing aspect of marriage is money.* As far as our possession of, attitude toward, and use of money are concerned, my wife and I are to be one flesh.
   3. To say that my wife and I are to be one flesh in the area of finances is a simple matter, but actually to bring it to pass may be very difficult.

B. In the course of my experience as a pastor-counselor, I have discovered that *the subject of finances can be one of the most divisive forces in marriage.* The husband has his ideas about money, and the wife has hers.
   1. He thinks that money is very important, and she does not think it is.
   2. She thinks they ought to save as much as they can for future needs and emergencies. He thinks they ought to use it as fast as they get it, and trust the Lord about the future.
   3. He wants to choose a job primarily on the basis of salary and other financial benefits. She thinks that other factors such as location, environment, proximity to their parents, a sound church, their friends, and a Christian school for the children ought seriously to be considered.
   4. He thinks they should give generously to the church, to needy people, to their parents and children. She thinks it is alright to give but is concerned about their own future needs and emergencies and advises caution and restraint in giving.
   5. He is inclined to spend money freely on amusements, entertainment, recreation, and vacations. She is more disposed to caution and re-

serve, believing that if you want exercise or diversion you can get it by mowing the lawn or gardening or doing something that does not cost money.

6. He wants to work as much as he can. He is glad for the opportunity for overtime or even a second job. After all, work is money, and the financial needs of his family are great. She, on the other hand, wants him to spend more time at home with her or with the children or doing the necessary chores and maintenance work. To her, good relations within the family require and should be given time. To her, what he sacrifices by working overtime or holding a second job is too valuable to give up. After all, money is not everything, and there are things that money cannot buy.

7. He has one idea about what is a financial priority, and she has another. He is convinced that they need to buy a new automobile, or at least a second automobile, right away. This is priority number one for him. She is just as convinced that they do not need another automobile. Their present automobile is working just fine. What they really need is a new dining room set or some new living room furniture. What they now have is at least ten years old. Anyone can see that it needs to be replaced. Why, imagine what people must think when they walk in and see their badly worn furniture!

C. Well, on and on we could go, describing various areas of potential marital conflict over finances.

1. These, however, are sufficient to illustrate the fact that especially if a couple does not have an abundance of money, the area of finances can be an area of serious conflict.

2. *It is very unlikely that a married couple will escape some conflict over finances,* first, because each of them is a sinner and therefore inclined to be selfish, second, because they have been raised in different homes and have consciously and unconsciously imbided attitudes and ideas about money from their parents. For years their parents have been teaching them either formally or informally about finances. Perhaps they did not accept everything their parents taught, but, like it or not, they were influenced by it. If the value systems of their respective parents were similar, their financial conflicts may be minimal. But if the parental value systems were quite different, unity in the area of finances may require a lot of prayer, study, and work. Indeed, the couple may discover that the area of finances is the area in which they have the greatest problem experiencing unity. They may discover that this is the area in which many a struggle occurs.

3. The question of how a married couple can achieve unity in the area of finances is not merely an academic, theoretical question. *It is a*

very practical question which throbs with life. It must be faced. It must be answered.

I. *Undoubtedly the foundation of financial unity in marriage is a mutual, sincere commitment to a biblical philosophy of money.* A Christian couple should accept a biblical philosophy of money, not merely because it works or because it produces unity, but because that is what God wants. However, they will discover that when they both take the Bible philosophy about money seriously, increasing unity will be a side benefit. Usually people have conflicts because they are operating according to different standards or ideas or value systems. Telling them to be united, making them feel guilty about their disagreements will not produce unity. As a rule, real unity will come only when they adopt a common standard or value system. In my opinion, most financial conflicts in marriage are caused by a lack of understanding of or submission to scriptural principles of money. In my opinion, most financial conflicts can be solved when both individuals really apply the biblical philosophy of money to their own lives. Let me then share with you some aspects of a biblical philosophy of money.

A. *God is the one who gives a man the ability to make money.* (The phrases which call particular attention to the biblical principle I am emphasizing are italicized. Scripture quotations are from the New American Standard Bible or the Amplified Bible, or are my paraphrases of these versions.)

1. Deuteronomy 8:18: "You shall earnestly remember the Lord your God; *for it is He who gives you power to get wealth. . . .*"

2. I Chronicles 29:11, 12: "Yours, O Lord, is the greatness, and the power, and the victory, and the majesty; . . . *both riches and honor come from You,* and You reign over all. In your hand are power and might; in your hand it is to make great and to give strength to all."

3. Proverbs 10:22: *"It is the blessing of the Lord that makes rich,* and He adds no sorrow to it."

4. I Corinthians 4:7: *"What have you that was not given you?* If you then received it, why do you boast as if you had not received it?"

B. *Everything we have belongs to God.*

1. Psalm 24:1: *"The earth is the Lord's and the fullness of it,* the world and they who dwell in it."

2. I Chronicles 29:11, 14: *"Yours, O Lord, is . . . all that is in the heavens and the earth. . . .* yours is the kingdom, O Lord, and yours it is to be exalted as head over all." "For all things come from you, and of your own hand we have given you." (Note the implications that principles A and B convey concerning the use of money. We are stewards of all we have. We must use our resources prayerfully and carefully, as He desires, not as we desire.)

C. *There are many things which are more valuable than gold.*

1. Matthew 16:26: "What will it profit a man if he gains the whole world, and forfeits *his soul?* Or what would a man give in exchange for *his soul?"*
2. Luke 12:15: "A *man's life* does not consist and is not derived from possessing overflowing abundance."
3. Proverbs 15:16, 17: "Better is little with the reverent, *worshipful fear of the Lord,* than great and rich treasure and trouble with it. Better is a dinner of herbs *where love is,* than a fatted ox and hatred with it."
4. Proverbs 16:8: "Better is a little with *righteousness*—uprightness in every area and human relationship and right standing with God—than great revenues with injustice."
5. Proverbs 16:16: "How much better it is to get *godly wisdom* than gold. And to get *understanding* is to be chosen rather than silver."
6. Proverbs 22:1: "A *good name* is rather to be chosen than great riches, and *loving favor* rather than silver and gold."
7. Jeremiah 9:23, 24: "Let not the person who is rich, glory and boast in his temporal satisfactions and earthly riches; but let him who glories glory in this, that *he understands and knows me,* that I am the Lord who practices lovingkindness, judgment, and righteousness in the earth; for in these things I delight, says the Lord."
8. Luke 12:20, 21: "But God said to him, You fool! This very night *your soul* is required of you; and all the things (material possessions) that you have prepared, whose will they be? So it is with him who continues to lay up possessions for himself and is not *rich in his relation to God."*
9. Matthew 6:19, 20: "Do not gather and heap up for yourselves treasures on earth . . . but gather and heap up and store for yourselves *treasures in heaven* where neither moth nor rust nor worms consume and destroy, and where thieves do not break through and steal."
10. I Timothy 6:6, 9: *"Godliness* accompanied with *contentment* is great and abundant gain." "But those who crave to be rich fall into temptation and a snare, and into many foolish and hurtful desires that plunge men into ruin and destruction and miserable perishing."
11. I Timothy 6:17, 18, 19: "As for the rich of this world, charge them not to be proud and arrogant and contemptuous of others, nor to set their hopes on uncertain riches . . . charge them to *do good,* to be rich in *good works,* to be *liberal and generous hearted, ready to share,* in this way laying up for themselves a *good foundation for the future. . . ."*
12. Philippians 3:7, 8, 9: "Whatever former things I had that might have been gains to me, I have come to consider as loss for Christ's sake.

Yes, furthermore I count everything as loss compared to the possession of the priceless privilege of *knowing Christ Jesus my Lord, and of progressively becoming more deeply acquainted with Him.* For His sake I have lost everything and consider it all to be mere rubbish that I may win *Christ,* and that I may (actually) be *found in Him,* not having any righteousness that can be called my own, based on my obedience to the law's demands, but possessing that (genuine righteousness) which comes through faith in *Christ."*

13. Ephesians 3:8: "To me, though I am the very least of all the saints this favor, privilege was granted: *to proclaim . . . the unending (boundless, exhaustless) riches of Christ."*

14. Psalm 19:9, 10; Psalm 119:72: *"The ordinances of the Lord* are . . . more to be desired than gold, even than much fine gold." *"The law of thy mouth* is better to me than thousands of gold and silver pieces."

15. Proverbs 19:1: "Better is a poor man who walks in his *integrity* than he who is perverse in speech and is a fool."

16. Proverbs 31:10; 19:14: *"An excellent wife,* who can find? For her worth is far above jewels. . . . he will have no lack of gain." "House and wealth are an inheritance from fathers, but a *prudent wife* is from the Lord."

17. Matthew 6:33; Colossians 3:1, 2: "Seek (aim at and strive for) first of all *His Kingdom,* and *His righteousness* (His way of doing and being right), and then all these things (your material needs) will be given you besides." "Aim at and seek *the things that are above,* where Christ is, seated at the right hand of God. And set your minds and keep them set on *what is above*—the higher things— not on the things that are on earth."

18. Psalm 127:3, 5: "Lo, *children are a heritage of the Lord,* the fruit of the womb a reward." "Happy, blessed, fortunate is the man whose quiver is filled with them." (Consider the implications of the fact that the things mentioned in these verses are more valuable than gold. What bearing does this have on the way we work, the job we take, the way we use our time, etc.?)

D. *Covetousness, discontentment, and worry about material things are sins.*

1. Exodus 20:17: *"You shall not covet your neighbor's house,* your neighbor's wife, or his manservant, or his maidservant, or his ox, or his donkey, or *anything that is your neighbor's."*

2. Colossians 3:5: "Therefore kill (deaden) the evil desire lurking in your members: sexual vice, impurity . . . and *all greed and covetousness,* for that is idolatry (the deifying of self or other created things instead of God)."

3. Hebrews 13:5: "Let your way of life be free from the love of money,

being content with what you have. . . ."

4. Luke 12:15: "Guard yourselves and *keep free from all covetousness* —the immoderate desire for wealth, the greedy longing to have more."

5. Matthew 6:25, 31, 34: "I tell you, *stop being perpetually uneasy about your life, what you shall eat or what you shall drink,* and about your body, what you shall put on." "Do not worry and be anxious, saying, What are we going to have to eat? or, What are we going to have to drink? or, What are we going to have to wear?" "So *do not worry or be anxious about tomorrow. . . .*" (Consider the implications of these verses in reference to keeping up with other people, longing after newer and brighter things, buying appliances, etc., which are not really necessary.)

E. *God expects us to use fully the strength and abilities He has given us in hard, honest work.* This is His normal way of supplying our needs. God usually rewards hard work with a measure of prosperity.

1. Exodus 20:9: *"Six days you shall labor* and do all your work."

2. Proverbs 13:11: "Wealth obtained by fraud, or unjustly, or from the production of things for vain or detrimental use, (such riches) will dwindle away; but *he who gathers by labor* (gradually) *will increase them."*

3. Proverbs 6:6, 9, 11: "Go to the ant, *you sluggard;* consider her ways, and be wise." "How long will you sleep, *O sluggard?* When will you arise from your sleep?" "So will your poverty come as a robber or one who travels, and your want as an armed man."

4. Proverbs 10:4: "He becomes poor who works with a slack and idle hand, but *the hand of the diligent makes rich."*

5. Proverbs 14:23: *"In all labor there is profit,* but idle talk leads only to poverty."

6. Proverbs 26:14: "As the door turns on its hinges, so does the lazy man on (move not from his place) his bed."

7. Ephesians 4:28: "Let the thief steal no more, but rather *let him be industrious, making an honest living. . . ."*

8. Colossians 3:23, 24: *"Whatever may be your task, work at it heartily, as (something done) for the Lord* and not for men, knowing (with all certainty) that it is from the Lord that you will receive the inheritance which is your real reward. You are actually serving the Lord Christ."

9. I Thessalonians 4:11, 12: *"Make it your ambition . . . to work* with your hands . . . so that you may bear yourselves becomingly . . . depending on nobody and having need of nothing."

10. Proverbs 28:22; 21:5; 28:20; 20:21: "He who has an evil and covetous eye hastens to be rich, and knows not that which will come

upon him." *"The thoughts of the (steadily) diligent tend only to plenteousness,* but everyone who is impatient and hasty hastens only to want." *"A faithful man shall abound with blessings;* but he who makes haste to be rich (at any cost) shall not be unpunished." "An inheritance hastily gotten (by greedy, unjust means) at the begining, in the end will not be blessed."

F. This series of verses under number 10 supports the principles suggested at the beginning of section D, namely that *God wants us to use our strength and abilities in honest, hard work and that this is His normal way of supplying our needs and that He usually rewards hard, honest work with some measure of prosperity.* However, they teach more than that. They also contain warnings about *the dangers of get rich quick schemes and excessive overtime or a second job.*

1. In our day, when men try to get rich quickly; when men neglect their own spiritual lives and their wives and their children and the church because they want to make more money, these verses need to be given serious consideration.

2. Many have ignored the instructions of these verses and are now suffering the consequences in the form of estrangement from God, wife, and children.

3. To be sure, hard, honest work is a command of God. But *if a man becomes so consumed with his work that he neglects other God-given privileges and responsibilities,* Proverbs says, *"He shall not be unpunished."*

G. *Giving to the Lord and to needy people is a privilege and an investment as well as a responsibility.*

1. II Corinthians 9:7: *"Let each one give* as he has made up his own mind and purposed in his heart, not reluctantly or sorrowfully or under compulsion, for God loves a cheerful (joyous, prompt-to-do-it) giver—whose heart is in his giving." "Remember this: . . . *he who sows generously* and that blessings may come to someone, *will also reap generously* and with blessing" (vs. 6).

2. Luke 6:38: *"Give and (gifts) will be given you,* good measure, pressed down, shaken together and running over. . . ."

3. Proverbs 14:21: "He who despises his neighbor sins, but *happy is he who is gracious to the poor."*

4. Proverbs 19:17: *"He who is gracious to a poor man lends to the Lord, and He will repay him for his good deed."*

5. Proverbs 22:9: *"He who is generous will be blessed,* for he gives some of his food to the poor."

6. Ephesians 4:28: "Let him labor, performing with his own hands what is good, in order that he may have something to *share with him who has need."*

7. Galatians 6:6: "Let him who receives instructions in the Word (of God) *share all good things with his teacher—contributing to his support.*"
H. *We ought to plan how we will make and spend our money.*
   1. Proverbs 20:18: *"Purposes and plans are established by counsel, and only with good advice make war."* This verse does not apply specifically to finances, but it does establish the need for planning important details.
   2. Proverbs 27:23, 24: *"Be diligent to know the state of your flocks, and look well to your herds; for riches are not forever;* does a crown endure to all generations?" The principle of planning and carefully superintending our resources is clearly taught by these verses.
   3. Luke 14:28 is not mainly referring to financial planning, but in this verse *Jesus does speak in favorable terms of the man who plans before he begins to build.*
   4. Luke 16:9-11: *"Make friends for yourself by means of unrighteous mammon (that is, money, possessions). . . . He who is faithful in a very little,* is faithful also in much. . . . Therefore if you have not been faithful in the (case of) money, possessions—who will entrust to you the true riches." The context and content of the verses encourage using wisdom and foresight in making and using money. It is true that our plans must be made prayerfully and judiciously, keeping in mind biblical principles. It is true that our plans must be submitted to the Lord, and we must be willing to adjust as He in His sovereignty either approves or denies. Concerning all of our plans, we must constantly say as James instructs us, "If the Lord wills, we shall live and also do this or that" (James 4:15). To do otherwise according to James is boasting in our "arrogance, presumption and self conceit. All such boasting is evil" (James 4:16). But though we must make our plans carefully and prayerfully and even then hold them with a light hand, still Scripture encourages us to make our plans.
I. *We ought to live within our income and not make debts which may be almost impossible to pay.*
   1. Proverbs 6:1, 2, 3: *"My son, if you have become security for your neighbor, if you have given pledge for a stranger or another,* you are snared with the words of your lips, you are caught in the speech of your mouth. Do this now, my son, and deliver your self. . . ." At first glance, this passage might be construed to mean that we should not help other people, but that is not the point of the passage at all. What the passage is warning against is putting yourself in a position where you may be obligated to pay a debt which is more than you can afford. The words "snared" and "caught" as well as the evident

84

urgency of the passage indicate that the obligation which is under consideration is a large one. It is one that may take you into bankruptcy or hinder you from fulfilling your other primary financial obligations to your God, your wife, and family. According to this passage, we should not make irresponsible financial commitments or debts which it would be difficult, if not impossible, to pay.

2. Proverbs 22:7: "The rich rules over the poor, and the borrower becomes the lender's slave." Other Scripture passages indicate that a certain amount of borrowing is legitimate. (Compare II Kings 4: 3: II Kings 6:5; Ex. 22:14, 15; Matt. 5:42; Matt. 21:1-3.) What this Scripture warns against is excessive borrowing, becoming so heavily indebted that you lose your freedom (financial and otherwise). Many couples have incurred so many debts from buying things they did not need or could not afford that they are literally the slaves of their creditors. This is wrong and ought to be avoided.

3. Romans 13:8: *"Render to all men their dues. Pay taxes to whom taxes are due, revenue to whom revenue is due. . . . Keep out of debt and owe no man anything. . . ."* In other words, do not make bills that you cannot pay, and pay all the bills that you do have.

These then are some aspects of a biblical philosophy of finances. They are the basic framework in which financial decisions should be made. They are the standards by which financial disputes and conflicts should be settled. In my opinion, the couple who will take these principles seriously and prayerfully try to apply them will be taking a big step in the direction of genuine unity in the marriage relationship.

II. Another giant step toward financial unity will come when the couple works out and applies the details of these principles in a very specific way to their own situation. Scripture says, "Faith without works (deeds and actions of obedience to back it up) by itself is destitute of power—unproductive, inoperative, barren, dead" (James 2:17). Likewise, a knowledge of and even mental assent to a biblical philosophy of money will be of little value unless the details are pointedly and specifically applied. A biblical philosophy of money is the foundation of the building and of fundamental importance to financial unity. Without a good foundation, you usually do not have a good building. But the foundation is not all there is to the building. It is only the beginning and unless the superstructure is built, the foundation is of little use. To implement these biblical principles about money, I make the following suggestions:

A. *Begin by realistically determining your income.*

1. Before you can determine how much you can send out, you need to know how much will be coming in. You cannot spend what you do not have.

85

2. To determine your income, make a list of all your monthly gains or profits. Include your salary, interest on savings accounts, stock dividends, what you make on side jobs, income from other members of the family, etc. (A form for doing a financial profile is included in the study section of this unit.)

B. Having determined your income, you may now go on to plan your outflow. (A form for this project is provided in the study section of this unit.)

1. *Right at the top of your list should be a generous portion for the ministries of your church.*

    a. Note I did not say a generous portion for the Lord, because I believe we should use all our money for the Lord. That is, we should use all our money in a way that God would approve. In that sense, all our money is to be given to the Lord. Stewardship is to be total, not partial.

    b. Yet the Scripture makes it clear that part of our money should be used to support the ministries of the church. (Compare Acts 6:4; I Corinthians 9:7-11, 13, 14; I Corinthians 15:57–16:2; Galatians 6:6-10; I Timothy 5:17, 18; Luke 10:1-7.)

    c. Good stewardship of our finances then will include setting aside a generous portion for the ministries of the church. This ought to be done regularly, consistently, cheerfully, thoughtfully, and proportionately.

    d. In my opinion, the idea that we should postpone generous giving until our debts are paid or until we get a raise or until the children are grown up or until we have bought a house is contrary to the Scripture. We may be able to give more then, but we ought to give generously now.

2. *Set aside the portion of money that is necessary to pay your taxes.*

    a. Add up all the taxes you will have to pay for the year. Break that amount down into 12 segments, and you have the portion you should save for taxes every month. (The amount withheld would be altered when the employer deducts your social security and income tax.)

    b. Compare Luke 3:7, 8, 13; Mark 12:17; and Romans 13:6, 7 to see how important it is for us to pay our taxes promptly.

3. *Make a detailed breakdown of all your family needs* (I Tim. 5:8). On your list of needs, you will probably want to plan for:

    a. House payments or rent
    b. Electricity, heat, water, telephone
    c. Food
    d. Automobile payments and maintenance
    e. Furniture and appliances

f. Clothing and its maintenance (cleaning, repairs)
g. Insurance needs
h. Regular payment of all outstanding debts
i. Doctor, dentist, and medicine bills
j. Hospitality (feeding and entertaining others)
k. Family recreation and vacations
l. Savings and investments (Generally, it is much better to save money and pay cash for purchases rather than borrow or charge. The interest rate on some charge accounts per year is more than 18 percent of the original amount. Sometimes, it may be necessary and wise to borrow or charge. However, you probably should not borrow money for an item unless the item is really needed and its purchase cannot be postponed until you could save the necessary amount. Nor should you borrow or charge unless you are sure you can add this debt to your present obligations and not become over-extended or burdened.)
m. Reading material (Christian literature, magazines, newspaper)
n. Education (your own and the children)
o. Helping others (meeting the necessities of the deprived saints and others)
p. Incidentals (haircuts, permanents, postage)
q. Gifts (birthdays, Christmas, weddings, baby showers, graduation)
r. Allowances (spending money for children, husband, wife)
s. Emergencies (new furnace, water heater, unexpected repairs, etc.)
4. At this point, you will need to compare your total monthly income with your monthly out-flow. If your financial out-flow is greater than your income, you must plan how to bring your income and expenditures into balance. I know of only two ways to do this.
   a. You could try to decrease your expenditures. Go back over your budget and ask:
      1) Is there anything on the list which is *totally unnecessary?*
      2) Is there anything we could use *less of?*
      3) Could we use a *substitute* or *cheaper item?*
      4) Is there *another way* of procuring the item?
      5) Could we *postpone* the purchase of the item?
      6) Is it something we could buy and *use along with someone else?*
      7) Do we have something that could be *sold and replaced* by a cheaper or smaller version?
   b. You could attempt to increase your income.
      1) If you work at a job where you are paid by the hour, you might increase your income by *working overtime.* Or you could find a *part-time second job.* Perhaps you could get a

regular Saturday morning job or pick up odd jobs as a handyman or doing lawn work. As indicated earlier, you must exercise caution in accepting overtime or taking a second job. You must have time to maintain your spiritual life, to relate to your family, and to take care of household and personal needs. If you do take a second job or accept overtime, you must schedule time for these other items and set a limit on the number of extra hours you will work. Whenever possible, take members of the family with you to do handy work or lawn work. At least, you will be with your family.

2) Calmly and respectfully confront your employer with your needs and *ask for a raise.* Do this only after much prayer. Make sure that you are the kind of loyal, dedicated, honest, respectful, hard-working employee that deserves a raise.

3) *Involve the wife or other members of the family in the work force.* (Compare Ps. 128:3; 127:4-6; Prov. 31:10-31.) One family has supplemented their income by cooperating in servicing several paper routes. Together they roll up the papers. Then mother drives the vehicle while the children throw the newspapers on the appropriate lawn. Actually this has become a family project. They are making money and building unity and relationships as well. Again, however, a word of caution is in order. If the wife becomes involved in the work force, she must not do so in such a way that her other responsibilities to God, husband, family, and herself are neglected. If the children become involved, similar caution must be exercised.

4) *Make a list of all your assets.* Are there items you have that you really do not need? *Could you sell them?* Check your attic or garage or basement. Could you have a lawn sale? Could you dispose of some antiques? Do you have duplicates of some things?

5) *Become a self producer.* Save money by learning to sew, knit, or do ceramics. Put out a garden, learn to do carpentry or fix your own car. If you become good enough at these things, you might earn extra income by doing them for other people. Many side lines have become profitable businesses.

6) Assuming you are qualified, *consider applying for a higher paying job or even changing jobs.* Do not be a job hopper, but if your education, experience, and abilities qualify you for more challenging and rewarding work, you may be justified in seeking it.

7) *Ask the advice of others* who have faced similar difficulties

88

and succeeded. Avoid being a "poor mouther" at all costs, but do not be ashamed to ask for advice and counsel. Someone else may know how to make a little go a long way or how to make more money without sacrificing other important responsibilities.

8) *Make your need of money and the administration of money a matter of believing prayer.* "The effective prayer of a righteous man can accomplish much" (James 5:16). "Lean on, trust in the Lord with all your heart, and do not rely on your own insight or understanding. In all your ways, recognize and acknowledge Him, and He will direct and make your paths straight" (Prov. 3:5, 6). "Trust in, lean on, rely on the Lord, and do good; so shall you dwell in the land, and truly you shall be fed" (Ps. 37:3). "My God will liberally supply your every need according to His riches in glory in Christ Jesus." If you honestly work as hard as you can, make as much as you can, and use what you have according to biblical principles, you can trust God to give you help with what is lacking. He was able to take care of Elijah during a time of great need. He fed the Israelites in the wilderness. He supplied the needs of Paul and Peter and Daniel. And He will help you as you trust and obey. "Jesus Christ is the same yesterday, today, and forever" (Heb. 13: 5). "He himself has said, I will not in any way fail nor give you up nor leave you without support. I will not in any degree leave you helpless, nor forsake you nor let you down— assuredly not" (Heb. 13:5, 6)! This is His promise, and you can depend on it.

III. Conclusion
   A. "For this cause shall a man leave his father and mother and shall cleave to his wife, and *they shall become one flesh"* (Gen. 2:24).
      1. Is that really possible?
      2. Can you experience genuine oneness in your marriage?
   B. Yes, you can if:
      1. Jesus Christ has set you free from the penalty and power of your sin. (Compare the conclusion of Unit 1.)
      2. You will accept and fulfill your respective roles in marriage. (See teaching material in Units 2 and 3.)
      3. You will develop and maintain a good communication system. (See teaching material in Unit 4.)
      4. You will adopt and apply the biblical principles of finances presented in this manual.

SUPPLEMENTARY READING FOR UNIT 5

Magic in Marriage, James H. Jauncey, Zondervan Publishing House, Grand Rapids, 1966, chapter 11.

How to Be Happy Though Married, Tim La Haye, Tyndale House Publishers, Wheaton, 1968, pp. 27-31.

Heaven Help the Home, Howard G. Hendricks, Victor Brooks, Wheaton, 1973, chapter 7.

Discovering the Intimate Marriage, R. C. Sproul, chapter 2.

Marriage Is for Love, Richard L. Strauss, chapter 12.

DISCUSSION AND STUDY QUESTIONS FOR UNIT 5
DEVELOPING FINANCIAL UNITY

To be completed together by husband and wife.

A. Study the following passages to discover how we should acquire, how we should regard, and how we should spend money.

1. Deuteronomy 8:17, 18 _____

2. I Chronicles 29:11, 12 _____

3. Ecclesiastes 5:19 _____

4. Ecclesiastes 5:10 _____

5. I Timothy 6:6-10 _____

6 I Timothy 6:17-19 _____

7. Luke 12:13-21 _____

8. Hebrews 13:5 _____

9. Philippians 4:11-19 _____

10. Proverbs 12:10 _____

11. Proverbs 11:28 _____

12. Proverbs 11:24, 25 _____

13. Proverbs 13:11; 14:23 _____

14. Proverbs 13:18, 22 _____

15. Proverbs 15:6 _____

16. Proverbs 15:16, 17, 22 _____

17. Proverbs 15:27 _____

18. Proverbs 16:8 _____

19. Proverbs 16:16 _____

20. Proverbs 20:4, 14, 18 _____

21. Proverbs 21:20, 25, 26 _____

22. Proverbs 22:1, 4, 7 _____

23. Proverbs 21:5, 6 _____

24. Proverbs 23:1-5 _____

25. Proverbs 24:30-35 _____

26. Proverbs 27:23, 24 _____

27. Proverbs 28:6, 22 _____

28. Proverbs 30:24, 25 _____

29. Matthew 6:19, 20 _____

30. Luke 6:27-38 _____

31. Ephesians 4:28 _____

32. II Thessalonians 3:7-12 _____

33. Romans 13:6-8 _____

34. Matthew 17:24-27 _____

35. Matthew 22:15-22 _____

36. Luke 14:28 _____

37. Proverbs 22:7 _____

38. Matthew 15:1-6 _____

39. Luke 16:10, 11 _____

40. II Corinthians 12:14 _____

41. I Timothy 5:8 _____

42. Acts 20:35 _____

43. Matthew 16:26 _____

44. Galatians 6:6; I Corinthians 9:11, 14 _____

45. II Corinthians 9:11, 14 _____

46. II Corinthians 9:6-12: List several principles of giving found in these verses.

    a. _____

    b. _____

    c. _____

    d. _____

    e. _____

    f. _____

47. Deuteronomy 15:10, 11 _____

48. I Corinthians 6:9, 10 _____

49. List the principles of giving suggested by I Corinthians 16:2.

    a. _____

b. _____

c. _____

d. _____

B. Make a list of principles from the previous verses that will guide you in your attitude toward, desire for, acquisition of, and use of money. Thirteen principles are already listed; you add your own insights to these principles. Put a circle around those principles which need to be implemented more fully in your life. Make them a matter of prayer.

1. *There are many things more valuable than gold* (Matt. 16:26; Luke 12:15; Prov. 15:16, 17).
2. *Covetousness and discontentment are sins* (Heb. 13:5; I Cor. 6:9, 10).
3. *God is the one who gives man the ability to make money* (Deut. 8:18; I Chron. 29:12).
4. *Heavenly treasure is to be more desired than earthly treasure* (Matt. 6: 19-20).
5. *God usually rewards hard work* (Prov. 13:11; 14:23).
6. *Everything I have belongs to God* (I Chron. 29:11). *Christian stewardship is total, not partial.*
7. *Giving to the Lord's work is a privilege and an investment, not merely a duty or obligation* (II Cor. 9:6-12; Phil. 4:11-19).
8. *I ought to save some of my income for future emergencies* (Prov. 30:24, 25; 13:22; 21:20).
9. *I must avoid get-rich-quick schemes* (Prov. 29:22; I Tim. 6:9; Prov. 13:11).
10. *I must not spend more than my income* (Rom. 13:8; Prov. 20:18; Luke 14:28).
11. *I must plan the way I use my income and discipline myself to use that plan* (Prov. 27:23-24; 16:10, 11).
12. *I ought to seek the counsel of wise men when I am about to make a major expenditure* (Prov. 20:18; 15:22).
13. *I ought to labor not simply that I might have, but primarily that I might give to others* (Eph. 4:28; Prov. 11:24).

14. _____

15. _____

16. _____

17. _____

18. _____

19. _____

20. _____

21. _____

22. _____

23. _____

24. _____

25. _____

C. Do a financial profile and make a budget.

  1. Assets
    a. Salary per month _____

    b. Additional income _____

             Total _____

  2. Liabilities
    a. Outstanding debts (total) _____

    b. Itemize regular monthly obligations

      1) Church—ministries _____

      2) Taxes _____

      3) Food and household items _____

      4) House payments or rent _____

      5) Electricity, heat, water, telephone ___

      6) Clothing and its maintenance ___

      7) Insurance _____

8) Recreation and vacation _____

9) Savings and investments _____

10) Payment of debts _____

11) Medical _____

12) Gifts _____

13) Hospitality _____

14) Reading material _____

15) Education _____

16) Allowances _____

17) Helping others _____

18) Emergencies _____

      Total _____

Compare total monthly assets with liabilities. If your liabilities are greater than your assets, you must plan how and when you will reduce your obligations or how you can increase your income. Decide what you will do and write out your plan.

_____

_____

_____

D. Discuss and seek a solution to the following matters.
   1. What will be your living standard? The husband's parents? The wife's parents? The neighbors? None of these?
   2. Will you engage in credit buying and charge accounts? If so, how much will you charge or buy on credit?
   3. What will you spend for recreation, gifts, and vacations?
   4. What will you give to the church? Will you give it all to the local church or to different Christian organizations?
   5. Will you make provision for your children's future education?
   6. Will you purchase insurance? If so, what kind? Life insurance, health insurance, home insurance, automobile insurance, etc.? And how much?
   7. Will you make out a will? Is it necessary?
   8. What about savings and investments? Will you have a savings account? Will you make investments? If so, where will you save or invest. And how much?
   9. Who will pay the bills and handle routine financial affairs? Who will be the treasurer of the family?
   10. How will you decide when to make major purchases such as another automobile or new furniture?
   11. How will you provide for emergencies?
   12. How will you provide for old age?
   13. Will the wife ever get a paying job?
   14. Will you borrow money? When? Where? How much?
   15. Will the husband take a second job?
   16. How often will you have people into your home for dinner?
   17. What do you do when you have a disagreement over the way the money is to be spent?
   18. Will you go out for dinner? How often?
   19. What attitudes did your parents have toward money? How did your respective parents differ in their attitude toward and use of money?
   20. What about personal allowances? Will each person have one? If so, how much? For what will the allowance be used?
   21. Will you buy a home or rent for the rest of your lives? If you buy, how much will you spend? What portion of your income will you spend on a home?
   22. What kind of appliances, equipment, and vehicles will you purchase?

96

UNIT 6

Developing Sexual Unity

In this unit, the problem of so-called "sexual problems" or "sexual incompatibility" is discussed. Some of the possible reasons for "sexual incompatibility," a biblical perspective on sex relations, and some pointed, practical suggestions for developing sexual unity are presented. Suggested supplementary reading, study questions, and exercises are included.

A. "For this cause shall a man leave his father and mother and shall cleave to his wife, and *the two shall become one flesh*" (Gen. 2:24).
   1. Every commentator that I studied on this passage agreed that *becoming one flesh is a broad concept involving the totality of life.* The context of Genesis 2 and the teaching of the rest of the Bible about marriage demand this.
   2. *At the same time, it is generally recognized that there is no place where this total sharing is more beautifully pictured or fully experienced than in the sexual relationship of the man and his wife.*
   3. In his book, *Design for Christian Marriage,* Dwight Harvey Small has written, *"Sexual intercourse is more than a physical act; it is a symbol of a spiritual relationship and the expression of the complete oneness of two persons in married love. . . . It is . . .* the means by which they are confirmed and nourished in that union. Sexual intercourse is the physical *establishment* and *confirmation of that oneness.* The true dignity of sex is in its ability to *enhance this personal unity* between two persons who have committed themselves to each other in love and marriage. In sexual intercourse the couple becomes joined in an indissoluble unity, called in the Bible "one flesh" (pp. 94, 96, emphasis added).
B. *Significantly, the Bible often describes the marriage act in terms of a man knowing his wife.*
   1. Genesis 4:1 is a case in point.
      a. The Amplified Version translates this verse, "And Adam knew Eve as his wife and she became pregnant."
      b. The New American Standard Version translates the Hebrew text, "Now the man had relations (the margin acknowledges that the word literally means knew) with his wife and she conceived."
   2. What else can this mean but that *the sex act is a means of deep communion and sharing* through which a husband and wife come to know each other in a very intimate way?

97

C. *Sexual relations are normally an integral part of genuine unity in marriage.*
  1. In the words of Dwight Hervey Small, they are a means of expressing, establishing, confirming, enhancing, and nourishing "the complete oneness of two persons in married love."
  2. According to the Bible, *the marriage act is more than a physical act. It is an act of sharing. It is an act of communion. It is an act of total self-giving* wherein the husband gives himself completely to the wife, and the wife gives herself to the husband in such a way that the two actually become one flesh.
  3. It becomes obvious, then, that the establishment of good sexual relations is an important part of developing genuine oneness in marriage.
D. Yet, it is sad but true that *there is no area over which more marital battles have been fought and more dissatisfaction manifested.*
  1. *Multitudes of couples have sought divorces, complaining of "sexual incompatibility."* A lawyer whom I interviewed told me that almost every couple who comes to him to get a divorce complains of "sexual incompatibility."
  2. And there are many couples who never seek a divorce who still have many a conflict over their sexual relations.
     My own personal experience as a counselor has certainly confirmed the fact that it is a major area of conflict. All too often the marriage act becomes a source of irritation instead of satisfaction; an area of conflict instead of a promoter and expression of unity.
  3. One question that must be faced is, *if God created and ordained sex relations as a promoter and expression of unity in marriage, why is it that many couples have problems in the area of sex?*
I. *Probably some couples have sexual problems because of unresolved guilt.*
   A. Scripture warns us to be sure that our sins will find us out (Num. 32:23). It also reminds us that we have a conscience that either "accuses or excuses us" (Rom. 2:15).
     1. We may try to ignore our sin. We may try to cover it up. We may even think we are doing a pretty good job of it.
     2. But we need to be sure that our sin will find us out. We have a conscience that frequently reminds us of our disobedience and prevents us from really enjoying life in the present.
     3. Witness the misery that David suffered because of unresolved sin and guilt in Psalm 32. He said, "When I kept silence (before I confessed), my bones wasted away through my roarings all the day long . . . my moisture was turned into the drought of summer" (Ps. 32:3, 4). In these words, David describes a horrible experience that he had as a result of unresolved guilt. He had grievously disobeyed God and then had tried to ignore his sin. But he could not

do it. To his dismay, he discovered that things which he once enjoyed, he no longer enjoyed. To his consternation, life began to lose its zest, and emotional, social, physical, and spiritual problems began to emerge. Why? Because God's hand of displeasure was heavy upon him. Because his conscience was constantly accusing him. Because his sins were finding him out.

B. In a similar fashion, *there are people who are presently having sexual problems in marriage because of unresolved guilt over illegitimate sexual experiences in the past.*

    1. I have had people tell me that they still felt guilty and were frequently disturbed about sexual sins they had committed seventeen or eighteen years before. Remembrances of past practices of heavy petting or self stimulation or homosexuality or promiscuous, selfish sexual practices continue to harass them, making it difficult to really enjoy proper sex relations now.

    2. R. C. Sproul writes, "Many women carry an enormous burden of guilt into marriage that festers for years. . . . One question I frequently ask men who complain to me about their wives' frigidity is, 'Did you have sexual relations with your wife before you were married?' . . . In every case where I have asked this question, the man has responded in the affirmative. Then I ask the next question: 'Would you say that your wife was more or less responsive to you sexually before you were married?' Again in every case where I have asked this question, the man has replied quite emphatically that his wife was indeed more responsive before they were married. Then they usually look at me with a puzzled glance and say, 'How did you know that?' The answer is that it is a rather common phenomenon. There can be many plausible explanations for the man's evaluation. . . . But one explanation should be given weighty consideration. Perhaps the woman feels so guilty about her loss of virginity before marriage that she is now suffering the paralyzing effects of that guilt" (*Discovering the Intimate Marriage,* pp. 96, 97).

C. Such a condition can be corrected *only when the person involved faces his sin, acknowledges it to God, seeks cleansing through the blood of Jesus Christ, depends upon the power of the Holy Spirit to change his attitudes and meditates on the Word of God.*

    1. "If we confess our sins, He is faithful and just to forgive us our sins and to cleanse us from all unrighteousness" (I John 1:9).

    2. "I acknowledged my sin to you, and my iniquity I did not hide. I said, I will confess my transgressions to the Lord (continually unfolding the past till all is told), then you forgave me the guilt and iniquity of my sin" (Ps. 32:5).

    3. "He who covers his transgressions will not prosper, but whoever

confesses and forsakes his sins shall obtain mercy" (Prov. 18:13).
4. "In whom we have redemption through His blood, the forgiveness of sins according to the riches of His grace" (Eph. 1:7).
5. "The blood of Jesus Christ His Son cleanses us from all sin and guilt" (I John 1:7).
6. "If anyone should sin, we have an advocate with the Father, Jesus Christ the righteous. And He is the propitiation (atoning sacrifice) for our sins . . ." (I John 2:1, 2).
7. "Do not be deceived; neither the impure and immoral, nor idolaters, nor adulterers, nor those who participate in homosexuality, will inherit the kingdom of God. And such were some of you. But you were washed clean (purified by a complete atonement for sin and made free from the guilt of sin) and you were sanctified (consecrated, set apart); and you were justified (pronounced righteous) in the name of the Lord Jesus Christ and by the Spirit of our God" (I Cor. 6:9-11).
8. "Now the Lord is the Spirit, and where the Spirit of the Lord is, there is liberty—emancipation from bondage, freedom. And all of us, as with unveiled face, beholding (perhaps this means contemplating in the Word of God or perhaps it means reflecting) as in a mirror the glory of the Lord, are constantly being changed into His very own image in ever increasing splendor and from one degree of glory to another; (for this comes) from the Lord who is the Spirit" (II Cor. 3:17, 18).
9. "How shall a young man cleanse his way? By taking heed and keeping watch according to your word. . . . Your word have I laid up in my heart, that I might not sin against you" (Ps. 119:9, 11).
10. "Oh, how I love your law! It is my meditation all the day" (Ps. 119:97).
11. "Let the Word of Christ dwell in your hearts (have its home in your hearts) in all its richness . . ." (Col. 3:16).
D. *Some couples could take a long step in the pathway to sexual adjustment by dealing with their sin in a biblical fashion.*
   1. I am not suggesting that a person should come to Christ or seek to obey Christ merely for the purpose of getting more enjoyment out of his sex life. God forbid that I ever should do that.
   2. *Man's basic problem is his alienation from God,* not the difficulties involved in sexual adjustment with his mate. Man is a sinner by nature and by practice (Jer. 17:9; Rom. 3:10-18; Ps. 51:5; 58:3; Eph. 2:1-3). His sins have separated him from his God. He is dead in trespasses and sins. He is under the curse and condemnation of God.
   3. *Man's greatest need is to be born again by the Spirit of God, to be*

100

reconciled to God, to be redeemed and forgiven, to be brought into the favor of God through the person and work of Jesus Christ. Man's great problem is sin, which alienates him from God. Man's great need is reconciliation to God through Jesus Christ. So man should come to Jesus Christ primarily for this reason (Eph. 2:4-7; Rom. 5:6-21; Col. 3:13-21).

4. However, *the Scripture does promise many side benefits to those who have been regenerated by the Holy Spirit and redeemed through Jesus Christ.* "Godliness is profitable in everything, for it holds promise for the present life and also for the life to come" (I Tim. 4:8). "I am come that they might have and enjoy life, and have it in abundance—to the full, till it overflows" (John 10:11). "God, who richly and ceaselessly provides us with everything for our enjoyment" (I Tim. 6:17). Certainly Wade Robinson was stating a scriptural truth when he said that for the Christian, "Heaven above is softer blue, Earth beneath is sweeter green, Something lives in every hue, Christless eyes have never seen."

5. I firmly believe that *a real Christian has the potential to enjoy the good things God has created for man more fully than the non-Christian.* Sex is one of the good things that God has created for man (Gen. 1:27-31; Heb. 13:4). I believe that the release, the enabling, the freedom from the penalty and power of sin that redemption brings can solve many of the sexual problems that couples face in marriage. It often happens that when couples get their relationship to God straightened out, their relationships with one another begin to straighten out as well.

II. *Many times, the sexual problems of married people are not really sexual problems.*

A. This may sound like double talk, but it is not. What I mean is that *poor sexual adjustment is often like the red warning light on the dashboard of an automobile.*

1. The red light is an indication that the car has some other problem or problems. Working with the red light (jiggling, shaking, banging) or even replacing it will not solve the automobile's real problems. You have to go deeper than that.

2. The red light indicates that the car needs oil or water, or that the brake needs to be released. Solve these problems, and the red light will go out automatically. Ignore these problems, and the red light will continue to glow until the automobile is ruined.

3. After years of study and experience in marriage counseling, James Petersen asserts, "Conflicts over money or religion, neglect or discourtesies, quarrels and bitter words will in time have an adverse effect on sexual harmony. One reason why it appears that sexual

adjustment is difficult to achieve is that failure in any one or several of the other major areas of marital life is reflected in physical relationships. Generally a couple which has achieved a satisfactory cooperative framework in which to face all their other problems will find a minimum of difficulty in coming together sexually" (quoted by Dwight Hervey Small in *After You've Said I Do,* p. 228).

B. I have heard Dr. Jay Adams graphically describe what I am talking about in this way. He compares the unresolved problems that couples may have to suitcases.

1. Here is a husband who does not love his wife in a biblical fashion. He's thoughtless, inconsiderate, harsh, ungrateful, irritable, unforgiving, impatient, and contentious. He bosses her around as though she were a slave, or ignores her as if she did not exist, or treats her as if she were an object instead of a real person.

2. The result? Why, the husband's attitudes and actions begin to weigh upon his wife. She thinks about them. She is hurt by them. She feels unwanted, unloved, unappreciated, and neglected. *They become like heavy suitcases that the wife carries around with her all the time.* They are with her when she is cooking or when she is cleaning, but *they are especially with her when she goes to bed with her husband.* There are the suitcases of his inconsideration, of his harshness, of his ingratitude, of his unforgiving spirit, of his unconfessed sin against her. There are the suitcases of her self pity and bitterness and resentment between them.

3. And then he turns to her and wants to have sexual intercourse. *They engage in the physical act, but both of them know that something is missing.* Somehow the marriage act has been hollow, empty, meaningless, and unfulfilling.

4. Why? The explanation is simple. *They have tried to have sexual relations in a bed piled high with suitcases between them.*

5. How do you solve the sexual problem in this case? *You solve it by getting rid of the suitcases.* The real problem in a situation like this is not the sexual problem. *The real problem is a host of other problems between the husband and wife.* Solve those problems, and it may well be that the sexual problems will be automatically corrected. Ignore those problems, and the sexual problems will probably get worse.

C. Colossians 3:12 tells us that *love is the perfect bond of unity.*

1. When applied to sexual relations in marriage, that verse speaks volumes. *If love is the perfect bond of unity, sexual problems may be the red light on the dashboard of the marriage indicating a lack of biblical love in that marriage.*

2. Usually when couples are expressing and experiencing I Corin-

thians 13 love, sexual problems are at a minimum. A fresh application of the type of love which is patient, kind, humble, compassionate, gentle, forgiving, unselfish, courteous, considerate, sensitive, truthful, appreciative, and protective will do more to improve sex relations than reading all of the latest books on methods and techniques. Let the husband and wife lovingly and joyfully fulfill their biblical roles toward each other; let them learn to communicate deeply according to biblical principles, and most of their sexual problems will evaporate.

III. At the same time, it must be acknowledged that *some sexual problems are the result of ignorance or misinformation.*

    A. *Some married people are woefully ignorant about their mate's physical anatomy.*

        1. One Christian man knew that his wife was not receiving personal pleasure from their marital relations. She dutifully submitted to him, but he began to feel guilty for "forcing" her to engage in an activity which was mostly for his satisfaction. She assured him that she was pleased to please him. Still he was concerned because he genuinely wanted to bring pleasure to her. He was convicted about selfishness. He made their sexual relations a matter of prayer.

        2. In the larger context of the marriage, he practiced consideration and did try to nourish and cherish his wife. Still, after fifteen years of marriage, his wife had never experienced a definite climax. Finally, he sought help, and when he did, he discovered that his inability to really please his wife was due to an ignorance of her sexual apparatus. As a result of some new information, this man and his wife, who both happen to be college graduates and very intelligent, began to experience a sexual unity which had previously been unknown.

    B. But if ignorance concerning the mate's physical anatomy is sometimes a problem, *ignorance concerning the mate's temperamental differences is more often a problem.*

        1. *Many women do not seem to understand the male temperament.*

            a. They do not comprehend that *most men are very easily and very quickly aroused.* Nor do they know that most men are stimulated by sight. Without even touching a woman's body, a man can be aroused. It can happen very easily.

            b. Perhaps this is why Jesus warned men about the danger of looking on women who are not their wives (Matt. 5:28). Perhaps it is because men are easily aroused that the book of Proverbs contains admonition after admonition to men concerning the danger of being seduced by loose women (Prov. 5:1-23; 6:23-35; 7:1-27).

c. Because men are easily aroused, they need to be very careful about what they look at and what they think about. On the other hand, women need to be careful about the way they dress and walk and talk before men who are not their husbands. In addition to this, wives must recognize that their husband's sexual desires are more quickly stimulated and, initially at least, more intense. *Wives must realize that their husbands may desire sexual relations more frequently than they do, and that this does not make them "sex perverts."*

d. Certainly, it is the husband's responsibility to exercise self control and to think in terms of his wife's condition and desires. But *it is also the wife's responsibility to be mindful of her husband's temperament and to seek to be his helper by being sensitive and willing to fulfill his sexual desires. Failure to understand the male temperament has tempted some women to harbor disrespectful and even resentful attitudes toward their husbands. Besides this, through ignorance these women have put an unnecessary burden of temptation upon their husbands.*

2. Unfortunately, ignorance concerning the varying temperaments of men and women is not restricted to the female gender.

a. *If anything, husbands are often more uninformed than wives.* Many a husband wrongly has accused his wife of being sexually cold and unresponsive, even "frigid." In his mind, he is a great "lover" and he cannot understand why his wife does not manifest the same interest in sex that he does. It must be that she is "undersexed" and he is sure that other women are much more interested in sex than is his wife.

b. *Actually, she is probably no different from most women.* As a rule, women are not aroused as easily as men. The sight of the male anatomy is not nearly as stimulating to a woman as is the sight of a woman to most men. *Soft words, unselfishness, consideration, genuine love, patience, kindness, appreciation, compassion, acceptance, and tenderness are the things that excite a woman* and prepare her for satisfying sex relations.

c. It is not true that she is less interested or incapable of enjoying sex as much as her husband. Rather, she is of a different temperament. She responds to other stimuli and in a different way. Consequently, if the husband wants his wife to enjoy "lovemaking," he will have to resist the temptation to rush.

d. Because of his temperament, he may be aroused quickly, but in most cases this will not be true of his wife. She will probably become excited very slowly, and thus the husband must exercise patience and self control. *He must deny himself for her sake and be more interested in fulfilling her needs than his own.*

e. Furthermore, *he must continuously treat his wife with kindness, and not just when he wants to "make love."* The husband who becomes tender and solicitous about his wife only at certain times will soon have a wife who feels used and abused, a wife who doubts the sincerity of her husband's love.

f. Scripture does teach that "the wife does not have authority or control over her own body, but the husband" (I Cor. 7:4). The wife must then yield to her husband gladly and seek to satisfy his needs. She is not to refuse her husband unless by mutual consent (I Cor. 7:5). On the other hand, *the husband must be very sensitive to his wife's temperament, needs, and desires. He must "dwell with his wife in an understanding way"* (I Pet. 3:7). He must love his wife as Christ loved the church (Eph. 5:25). He must esteem his wife better than himself and be concerned about her interests as well as his own (Phil. 2:3, 4). He must give honor to her as the weaker vessel (I Pet. 3:7). He must make it his practice to please his wife for her good and not to please himself (Rom. 15:1, 2).

g. When the husband disregards this God-prescribed way of treating his wife, he is, of course, being disobedient to God. But he is also manifesting his ignorance of his wife's temperament. God's commands to husbands are in accordance with the woman's temperament. Thus, the husband who ignores God's injunctions is making it difficult for his wife to become genuinely one with him. Contrariwise, because these commands are in keeping with the woman's temperament, the husband who obeys them will be providing an atmosphere in which sexual unity and every other kind of unity will flourish.

C. One other kind of ignorance which sometimes causes sexual problems needs to be mentioned—namely, *ignorance of what the Bible has to say about sex.* Many people have the idea that the Bible really does not have much to say about sex and that what it does have to say is in a negative vein. On one occasion, I was staying in a pastor's home while conducting a Christian Home Seminar. One day we were sitting around the table having a cup of coffee and discussing various issues about marriage and the family. In the course of our conversation, this couple shared with me the fact that they had had some problems in adjusting to each other sexually. The woman had been raised in a home where nothing positive was ever said about sex and in a church where whatever teaching was given was always negative. As a result, the thought of sex was frightening to her. She got the idea that sex was something that women endured for the sake of procreation, but it certainly was not something that spiritual people ever discussed or enjoyed. Her home and her church had emphasized the abuse and wrong use of sex, but had failed to communicate to her the many positive things the Bible has to say about it. Surely their reason for emphasizing the Bible's negative teachings concerning the evil of pre-marital sex, masturbation, homosexuality, and adultery was good. They wanted to protect their youth from sin. However, at least in this woman's case, their failure to emphasize the Bible's positive teachings about sex had made it difficult for this woman to think of sex as anything but unspiritual and even dirty. Ignorance then of the Bible's positive teaching can produce sexual problems in marriage and hinder the genuine experience of oneness.

At this point, I want to share with you the seven important biblical principles concerning sexual relations which are delineated by Harry H. McGee, M.D., in the booklet, *The Scriptures, Sex, and Satisfaction*. These seven principles are taken from one pivotal passage in I Corinthians 7:1-6, but they are supported by many other passages as well.

1. *Sexual relations within marriage are holy and good* (Heb. 13:4). God encourages sexual relations and warns against the temptations that may arise from deprivation or cessation.

2. *Pleasure in sexual relations (like pleasure in eating or in the performance of other bodily functions) is not forbidden but rather assumed* when Paul writes that the bodies of both parties belong to one another (cf. also Prov. 5:18, 19 and Song of Solomon).

3. *Sexual pleasure is to be regulated by the key principle that one's sexuality does not exist for himself or for his own pleasure, but for his partner* ("rights" over one's body are given in marriage to one's partner). Every self-oriented manifestation of sex is sinful and lustful rather than holy and loving. Homosexuality and masturbation thereby are condemned along with other self-oriented activities within marriage. In sex as in every other aspect of life, it is "more blessed to give than to receive." The greatest pleasure comes from satisfying one's spouse.

4. *Sexual relations are to be regular and continuous.* No exact number of times per week is advised, but the principle that both parties are to provide such adequate satisfaction that both "burning" (unfulfilled sexual desire) and the temptation to find satisfaction elsewhere are avoided.

5. *The principle of mutual satisfaction means that each party is to provide the sexual enjoyment which is "due" his or her spouse whenever needed.* But, of course, other biblical principles (e.g., the principle of moderation), and the principle that one never seeks to satisfy himself but his partner in marriage always regulates the frequency in such a way that no one ever makes unreasonable demands upon

another. Requests for sexual satisfaction may never be governed by an idolatrous lust, but neither may such regulation be used as an excuse for failing to sense and satisfy a partner's genuine need.

6. In accordance with the principle of "rights," *there is to be no sexual bargaining.* ("I'll not have relations unless you. . . .") Neither partner has the right to make such bargains.

7. *Sexual relationships are equal and reciprocal.* Paul does not give the man rights superior to the rights of the woman. Mutual initiation of intercourse, stimulation, foreplay, and participation in the sexual act is not only permissible but enjoined. Marital rights entail mutual responsibility. (Quoted from the appendix of *The Scriptures, Sex and Satisfaction,* by Harry M. McGee, M.D. The appendix was written by Jay E. Adams.)

These then are some biblical principles concerning sex relations. I suggest that knowing and practicing them and other biblical principles found in this unit of this manual will help you to develop and maintain real unity in your marriage relationship.

SUPPLEMENTARY READING FOR UNIT 6

The Scriptures, Sex and Satisfaction, Harry McGee, M.D., Presbyterian and Reformed Publishing Co., Nutley, N. J., 1975.
Sexual Happiness in Marriage, Herbert J. Miles, Zondervan, Grand Rapids, 1967.
Physical Unity in Marriage, Shirley Rice, Norfolk Christian Schools, Norfolk, 1973.
Design for Christian Marriage, Dwight Small, chapters 4 and 5.
Discovering the Intimate Marriage, R. C. Sproul, chapter 4.
Marriage Is for Love, Richard L. Strauss, chapter 13.

DISCUSSION AND STUDY QUESTIONS FOR UNIT 6
DEVELOPING SEXUAL UNITY

To be completed together by husband and wife.

A. Read I Corinthians 7:2-5, 9 and list everything that you see in this passage about sex. Look for answers to such questions as—With whom is it proper to have sexual relations? What are the "marriage rights" of each partner in marriage? What are some of the purposes of marriage and of sexual relations? What attitude should both partners have about sexual relations? Is it proper for a Christian to masturbate? What is God's answer to sexual desire? Should

107

husbands and wives discuss their sexual relations and desires? How long should a couple refrain from sexual relations?

1. _____

2. _____

3. _____

4. _____

5. _____

6. _____

7. _____

8. _____

9. _____

10. _____

B. What does Proverbs 5:15-21 tell us about marriage and sexual relations?

1. _____

2. _____

3. _____

4. _____

5. _____

C. Summarize in a few sentences what principle Acts 20:35 might suggest concerning the sex act.

_____

_____

_____

_____

_____

D. Comparing I Corinthians 7:2-5, Proverbs 5:15-19, and Genesis 1:27, 28, list the purposes of sex in marriage.

1. _____

2. _____

3. _____

E. Paraphrase Hebrews 13:4 in your own words.

_____

_____

_____

F. What truths about the marriage relationship are taught in Malachi 2:13-16?

1. _____

2. _____

3. _____

4. _____

G. Study Philippians 2:3, 4 and state specifically how this passage may be applied to marital (sexual) relations.

1. _____

2. _____

3. _____

4. _____

H. What does Song of Solomon 1:2, 13-16; 7:1-10 teach us about the marriage relationship?

1. _____

2. _____

3. _____

4. _____

I. What attitudes toward the marriage partner and his/her body are suggested by the Song of Solomon 4:1-7 and 5:10-16? Should a marriage partner be embarrassed or ashamed because he finds delight in his partner? Is it proper to be excited about, to anticipate, and enjoy sexual relations with your spouse?

1. _____

2. _____

3. _____

4. _____

J. Look at I Corinthians 6:12; Matthew 5:27, 28; I Corinthians 7:9; and I Corinthians 7:3, 4, and list 4 reasons why masturbation is wrong.

1. _____

2. _____

3. _____

4. _____

K. What implications does the fact that I Corinthians 7:2-5 and Proverbs 5:15-19 indicate that begetting children is not the only purpose of the sex act have in reference to birth control?

1. _____

2. _____

3. _____

4. _____

5. _____

L. What relevance do I Timothy 5:8; Philippians 2:4; Ephesians 5:25, 28-29; I Corinthians 7:3, 5; Exodus 20:13; Genesis 1:27, 28; Proverbs 5:18-20; and James 2:17, 20 have in reference to birth control?

1. _____

2. _____

3. _____

4. _____

M. List 4 different methods of birth control.

1. _____

2. _____

3. _____

4. _____

N. According to Matthew 5:27-30 and Hebrews 13:4, how serious is the sin of sexual relations outside of marriage?

_____

_____

_____

_____

O. Discuss the following questions:
1. What pleases you about your present sexual relations?
2. Is there anything about your sexual relations you do not enjoy? When? How? Frequency? etc.?
3. What are the greatest hindrances to good sexual relations?
4. What is proper and improper in sexual relations? What does the Bible prohibit?

5. Does the pattern of your sex life need to be varied? If so, how?
6. How do you differ from your mate in your sexual attitudes, feelings, needs, desires?
7. Do you have any fears about sex? If so, what are they?
8. Do you communicate freely with your spouse about your sexual relations?
9. Does great sexual desire indicate a lack of spirituality?
10. How often should you have sex relations?
11. Should sexual relations be a mutually satisfying experience? What should you do if they are not? How will you get help if you are having problems achieving sexual adjustment?
12. What can you do to meet the sexual needs of your spouse more fully?

Unity Developed Through a Common Philosophy of Raising Children

In this unit another of the major areas in which unity may be either enhanced or thwarted is discussed. Biblical principles of child raising, suggested supplementary reading, study questions, and action plans which will make child raising a unifying rather than a divisive force are presented. Thirty-four practical, specific "how to" suggestions which may serve as a guideline and checklist are included in the study section of this unit.

A. Strange as it may seem, it is nonetheless true that the same sun produces different, even opposite results on different substances.
   1. It hardens clay but melts ice.
   2. It promotes health in human beings but kills germs.
   3. It tans or burns our skin but makes white cloth whiter.
B. And, strange as it may seem, it is nonetheless true that *children can be a magnetic force drawing married people together or a wedge which drives them apart.*
   1. As I did research for this manual I interviewed a variety of Christian people to find out what factors encouraged marital unity and what factors hindered marital unity. It soon became evident that the same things which promoted unity often were the very things that caused the greatest friction and conflict.
   2. Several people mentioned children as one of the greatest unifying factors in their marriage. Others indicated they had more serious disagreements over the children than over any other subject. In fact, one man told me that the only matter over which he and his wife ever argued was the children. He said, "We get along beautifully on almost everything, but when it comes to the children she often has her ideas and I have mine."
   3. To some people who have no children, it may come as a surprise that children could be an area of conflict for married people. Actually, however, *the potential for disagreements over children is enormous.*
      a. For one thing, *they may disagree over whether or not they should have any children.* He may want to have children, and she may not. Perhaps she does not want to be tied down, or she may not want to endure the pain of childbirth.
      b. *Or they may have differing views about when to have children.*

113

He may want to postpone having children until they have more money in the bank, or he has a better job. She may want to have children immediately because her girl friends already have children, and she feels unfulfilled without at least one child.

    c. Still further, *they may be at odds about how many children they should have.* He may want a whole litter and talk about having his own football team. She says, "Nothing doing. I love children, but I'm the one who has to bear them, feed them, diaper them, cook, wash, and clean for them. I want only two or three."

    d. *Probably the greatest conflicts over children come because the couple disagrees about how to raise the children.* In my experience this is the arena in which most of the struggles occur. In comparison to differences of opinion about how children should be raised, all other disagreements are very insignificant. He may think that the rod should be used frequently and forcefully. She may think that the use of the rod is brutal, cruel, and barbaric. He may think that the child should be given little freedom. He may believe that the child should learn to respect authority, that he needs order and structure, that he must learn to control himself from his earliest years. Conversely, she may be afraid of squelching the child's creativity and initiative. She believes the child needs to be disciplined, but she does not want her child to be repressed and inhibited. He may have one idea about chores and responsibility. In his estimation, children need to learn to carry part of the load, to toil by the sweat of their own brow, to serve others at an early age. She thinks that children should be allowed to spend their time in play. They will have the rest of their lives to work. And besides, it is easier to do it yourself than to make them do it. Her parents never forced her to do a lot of chores and she turned out all right.

4. Well, on and on we could go mentioning possible differences of opinion about how to raise children. These, however, are enough to illustrate the reality and the nature of some child raising disagreements.

C. I am convinced that many husbands and wives, even Christian husbands and wives, are working at cross purposes because they do not have any basic philosophy of children.

1. If you ask them, "What is your basic philosophy concerning your children?" they respond, "Basic philosophy? What in the world is that?"

2. You see, they have never really thought about the questions—Why do we want children? What should be our goals for our children? What are our responsibilities to our children? How should we raise

114

our children? Why do we do what we do in reference to our children?

3. They have no clearly defined goals or plans or strategy or standard to guide them in their child raising efforts. They just shoot from the hip. He does his thing and she does hers. And they do it that way because that is the way they feel about it, or that is the way their parents did it. They do not know why they do what they do. They do not know what they are trying to accomplish, and it is no wonder that they have conflicts.

D. Most serious conflicts could be eliminated for Christian couples *if they would really make the Bible their final authority on raising children.*

1. God who is our creator and the creator of our children; God who is all wise; God who knows the end from the beginning has given us in His Word clear directives concerning our parental responsibilities.

2. In His Word, He has given us a basic philosophy of child raising. In the Scriptures He has delineated for us the goals, the plans, the strategy, the standards by which we should raise our children. We do not need to shoot from the hip; we do not need to fly by the seat of our pants; we do not need to lean to our own understanding or the understanding of other fallible men in this matter.

3. We have the infallible Word of God to answer our questions, settle our disputes, and be our guide. Conflicts, disagreements, differences of opinion can be settled by couples who are willing to make the Word of God, not their own ideas or feelings or opinions, their final authority in the matter of raising children.

4. To me personally, one of the most profound and comprehensive, instructive and helpful verses in all of the Bible on the subject of children is Ephesians 6:4.

   a. In this verse God says, "Fathers, do not provoke your children to wrath; instead, bring them up in the discipline or training and instruction or counsel of the Lord."

   b. Here, in a very short space, God lays out for us a very comprehensive program; a basic philosophy of child raising. Here God tells us what not to do, what we should do, and what our goals and plans and strategy and methods and standards should be.

   c. I suggest that if a married couple thoroughly and mutually understand and apply the principles of this verse to their child-raising efforts, they will be good parents. But more than that, they will be united parents.

I. As we study this key verse on child raising, *we must not overlook the fact that it is particularly directed to fathers.*

A. Comparing Scripture with Scripture indicates that *the mother may be and should be actively involved in bringing up the children.*

115

1. Exodus 20:12 commands children to honor their fathers and mothers. In God's eyes the mother must be honored just as much as the father.
2. Proverbs 1:8 puts the mother right into the child raising process. It says, "My son, hear the instruction of your father, and forsake not the law of your mother."
3. Proverbs 6:20 speaks to the same issue. "My son," it reads, "keep your father's commandments, and forsake not the law of your mother."
4. I Timothy 5:10 asserts that women who have brought up children are qualified for special treatment when they are over sixty and widowed.
5. Assuredly, Scripture teaches that *women not only may, but must be involved in raising their children.* It is not the exclusive job of the father.
   a. Actually, common sense indicates that even if you wanted to, you could not keep the mother out of the child raising endeavor.
   b. As a rule, the children are with the mother much more than with the father. She is the one whose words they hear and whose example they see much more than the father's. She is the one who is usually available at the most teachable moments. She is ordinarily there when the children get up, when they eat breakfast, when they go to school, when they come home from school, when they play, when they get hurt, when they cry, when they laugh, when they go to bed. She is frequently present when they need rebuke, when they need instruction, when they need appreciation and acceptance and encouragement. Generally, she is on hand when they are rebellious or fearful or distraught.
   c. When all is said and done, the mother probably has more opportunities, more direct influence in the lives of the children than anyone. Think of the influence, the contribution that godly Hannah made to the life of Samuel. Consider the impact the mother of James and John made on their lives. Ponder the influence of Lois and Eunice in the life of Timothy. In a very real sense the old adage which declares that "the hand that rocks the cradle rules the world" is true. Of one thing you can be sure, mothers should be, must be, and are included in bringing up children.
B. Assuming that this is true, *why then does the Bible speak particularly to the father* in Ephesians 6:4?
   1. One possible explanation for this may be that *often it is the father who neglects this responsibility.* Many a man has transferred most of the child raising responsibilities to his wife.
      a. *In some instances, the husband has literally done this by telling*

116

the wife that "the kids" are her responsibility. His philosophy is that he will make the money and provide for their physical needs. She will take care of the home and the children. He will not expect her to do his work, and she should not expect him to do hers.

b. *In other cases, this has happened by default.* He becomes so involved in his work or at church or in some other activity that he does not "have time" to help with the children. I mean he hardly ever sees the children. He is almost never at home. And when he is, he does not want to be bothered by petty details. He thinks that he has enough trouble solving the problems he faces on his job or in the church or in his tennis game without being confronted with difficulties at home. After all, he reasons, a man can take only so much. Oh, it's not that he is not concerned, and he does love his children, but no man has the time and energy to do everything. Besides, the wife has plenty of time, and she is better with children anyway.

c. Well, with such rationalizations, or even without them, many a husband has salved his conscience and abdicated his child raising responsibility. But God says, "No, you fathers are to be involved in raising the children. You cannot transfer this job to your wives."

2. This, then, may be one explanation for the emphasis on fathers in Ephesians 6:4. Probably, however, the main reason for this approach is found in *the biblical doctrine of the husband's headship in the home.*

a. Jay Adams says, "When Paul speaks to the fathers he is speaking to the mothers. The reason that he addresses the fathers is that what the mothers do, the fathers are responsible for. In addressing the father, he is addressing the one in whom God has vested His authority for discipline. The father is the head of the home. The father is the one who ultimately must answer to God for what happens in the home" (*Christian Living in the Home,* p. 104).

b. When it comes to the home, the "buck" stops with the father. He is the one who is charged with the overall direction of the home. Ultimately, under God, he is the one who is responsible for authority, for guidance, for direction, for training, for discipline, for provision, and for raising the children. And he will be held accountable by God. He cannot relinquish this obligation unless he is incapacitated by illness or some other difficulty.

C. As previously stated, *this does not mean that the mother is pushed out of the picture.* Nor does it imply that her role is unimportant.

1. Three verses of Scripture in 1 Timothy 3 designate the husband as the manager of the home (vss. 4, 5, 12). This designation is tremendously significant.
   a. *A good manager knows the skills, the resources, the needs,* the potential, the weaknesses, the problems of the people or business he is managing.
   b. *A good manager knows how to use the skills and resources of his company.* He knows how to solve problems, how to draw the best out of people, how to encourage initiative and creativity, how to delegate responsibility.
   c. *A good manager is not a man who does the work of ten men.* He is a man who helps ten men do their best work. He does not do all the work himself. He enlists the help of others. Ultimately, he is responsible to see that the work gets done, but in accomplishing the job he welcomes all the assistance he can get.
2. *In the home, the husband must not neglect his ultimate responsibility for the children.*
   a. At the same time, he must learn how effectively to encourage, deploy, enlist, direct, and use every legitimate resource at his disposal to accomplish God's purpose for his children.
   b. Certainly, *his most important resource in accomplishing this task is his wife. God gave him his wife to be his suitable helper.* She is to be his chief consultant, resource person, and assistant. He must encourage her initiative and creativity. He must welcome her suggestions and advice. He must delegate authority and responsibility to her and give her freedom to express them. He must hold her up before the children as one to be honored, respected, heard, and obeyed.
   c. He and his wife are a team. *The goal toward which they are striving is the proper raising of children.* Together they must press toward that goal. The task is so great, the problems so many, the opposition so strong that mutual effort and cooperation will be required. The husband simply cannot do it alone. He needs to work as part of a team. He must have the full assistance of his wife. But *he is the team leader, and as such he is finally responsible.* (Consider the implications that this concept has for husbands, wives, children, the church, and society when a married couple really puts it into practice. Imagine the security, stability, progress, harmony, and unity that real obedience to this concept would bring. Perhaps this would be a good time to stop and discuss your own marriage in the light of this principle. What are its implications for you as a husband? Are there any changes you need to make? What are the implications of this

118

principle for you as a wife? Are there any changes that you need to make?)

II. Several other important facets of a biblical approach to child raising are expressed by the words "bring them up."

   A. In the Greek text the verb translated "bring up" is in the active voice, imperative mood and present tense.

      1. The active voice indicates that *children do not automatically grow up to be what God wants them to be.*

         a. It also implies that they cannot bring themselves up properly. This cannot happen because God says "foolishness is bound up in the heart of a child" (Prov. 22:15), and that "a child left to himself, a child who gets his own way brings shame to his mother" (Prov. 29:15).

         b. Scripture thus asserts that if you allow a child to bring himself up, if you raise him in an atmosphere of complete freedom, if you allow him to make all his own choices, to do his own thing, to express himself freely, the result will be shameful.

         c. God never intended children to bring themselves up. He gave them parents who are to be actively engaged in making the children what God wants them to be.

      2. In addition to being in the active voice, *it is significant that the Greek verb is in the imperative mood.*

         a. On occasion when we have not known what to do, most of us have turned to others for help. Sometimes they have replied by saying, "I am not going to tell you what to do, but if I were in your situation I would. . . ." In other words, the person has given us some friendly advice which we can take or leave.

         b. Well, *what God says in Ephesians 6:4 is not just friendly advice.*

            1) It is not just a suggestion that He hopes we will consider. *It is a command which He expects us to obey.*

            2) It is not one of many alternatives or options from which we may choose the way that we will raise our children. *It is the only option open to us as Christians.* This is the only way for us to raise our children. Disregard for these directives is not merely a mistake or a blunder. It is disobedience or rebellion against God, for He commands us to raise our children this way. The verb is in the imperative mood.

      3. Besides being in the active voice and imperative mood, *this verb is in the present tense.*

         a. At certain times in our parenting experience, I have looked at my wife and said, "I know the Lord says that children are the heritage of the Lord and the fruit of the womb is His reward (Ps. 27:3), but right now they do not seem like much of a reward.

It is a joy to have children, but wouldn't it be nice to be able to take a little vacation from responsibility? Wouldn't it be nice to be able to sit back for a month or two, and let the children be solely in charge of raising themselves, correcting themselves, and providing for themselves?"

b. But God says, "No, you cannot do that. As long as the children are in your home, you must be constantly, persistently, unremittingly bringing them up. This is not a job that you will do in a day or a month or a year or even ten years. It is a task that will take much time and constant effort. *It is a present task, not a past or future tense task.* It is not a job that ended yesterday. Nor is it a job that you can put off until tomorrow. As long as the children are under your care, every day will hold new opportunities for bringing them up."

1) I am not suggesting that parents should smother their children and give them no freedom. Smothering is almost as dangerous and disastrous as total permissiveness. It promotes hostility, insecurity, anxiety, resentment, overdependence, emotional instability, attitudes of inferiority, and undecisiveness. Nor am I recommending that the child should be expected to be perfect. He must be allowed to make mistakes and to fail without being given the impression that he has been rejected or that he is worthless.

2) Yet his serious defects and failures cannot be totally ignored. In the right way and at the right time he must be corrected and helped to improve.

c. God gives to parents the challenging task of bringing their children up. And the present tense of the verb "bring up" indicates that this is a task in which parents must be constantly involved. This is a job from which they are never off duty. *No time of day or night, no circumstance or situation or place is "off limits" for the performance of this task.*

B. Now all of this helpful and challenging information is compacted into the words "bring them up," *but there is still more to be found in these words.* Notice that God does not say, "Put them down, hold them down or in or back." Rather He says, "Bring them *up*. . . ."

1. We are to bring our children up *to know and trust in Jesus Christ* (Mark 10:13, 14; Matt. 28:19; Ps. 34:11).

2. But more than that, we are to bring our children up to be *real disciples of Jesus Christ* (James 1:21-25; Ps. 1:1-3; 119:9, 11, 105).

a. Our goal should be to bring our children to the place where they are disciplined in the way of the Lord so that their attitudes and patterns and way of life begin to reflect the likeness of Jesus Christ.

b. Our objective should be to so train them that their thoughts and attitudes and actions begin to reflect and manifest a likeness to the lifestyle of a Christian described in the Word of God. Whether they become successful in business, whether they become good athletes or musicians, whether they are handsome or beautiful, whether they get straight A's in school are matters of little consequence in comparison with the matter of becoming holy and godly and mature Christians.

c. Becoming mature Christians will require the sovereign work of God. Only God can save and sanctify. Still, God uses men and means. Certainly we as parents must seek to bring our children to Jesus Christ for salvation. But salvation is not the end of the journey. It is only the beginning. The destination toward which we are headed with our children is nothing less than maturity in Christ, the maturity described in the beatitudes and the rest of the Sermon on the Mount, in I Corinthians 13, in Ephesians 4–6, in Romans 12–15, and many other passages of Scripture. We should endeavor to bring our children up not only to know the truth, but to do it; to not only know what is right, but to do it. We should seek to bring our children up to live God-honoring lives, to be the light of the world, the salt of the earth, exerting a positive, overcoming, transforming influence in this world.

d. In the great commission, Jesus said, "Go and make disciples of all the nations . . . teaching them to obey everything that I have commanded you" (Matt. 28:19, 20). Notice that Jesus did not merely say, "Go and solicit decisions." Rather, He said, "Go and make disciples. . . ." Nor did He simply say, "teaching them to know everything that I have commanded you." What He actually said was, "Teaching them to observe, to obey, to practice everything that I have commanded you." Knowledge of facts is important. Knowledge of truth is essential. Yet our Lord's concern goes beyond mere head knowledge. He wants us to not only know the truth but obey the truth. He wants us to live the truth, practice the truth, and be conformed to and transformed by that truth. Our goal then as parents must be to bring our children up to obey the truth.

3. Surely the words "bring them up" convey the thought that we should try to prepare our children to leave the home nest and fly successfully for themselves. Our goal should be to bring our children to the place where they can make intelligent, biblical decisions for themselves, rather than depend on us for direction. Our objective

should be friendly separation and independence from us, not slavish dependence and attachment to us. Our target should be to see our children become primarily dependent on Christ and His Word, secondarily dependent on their married partners, and only casually dependent on us. (Consider the implications that this clearly defined goal for child raising has for your marriage. Is this your goal for your children? Are you really aiming at and working toward it? Ponder the harmony and unity that mutual commitment to the same goal would produce in a marriage. Agreement concerning your parental destination or goal will be a great unifying factor in your marriage. Perhaps this would be a good time to stop and discuss your overall goal as well as specific goals for your children.)

III. Now that is the goal toward which we as parents should press. But how is this goal to be realized? What strategy or methods should we use in trying to bring our children to that goal? Turning to our key text in Ephesians 6:4, we find a threefold answer to that question. One part of that answer is cast in a negative way as God tells us what to avoid in bringing up our children. Two parts of that answer are put in a positive form as God tells us what we should do.

A. *Negatively, God says that we must avoid provoking our children to wrath.*

1. At this point an explanation of the words "provoke" and "wrath" is in order, lest we completely misconstrue what this phrase teaches.

   a. To avoid provoking our children to wrath does not mean that we never do anything that would upset or annoy or make our children angry. It does not imply that we must never cross our children or withhold from them something that they desperately want.

   b. What it does connote is that we should not treat them in such a way that their passions are unnecessarily aroused. What it does mean is that *we should not handle them in such a way that they will be incited to a wrathful kind of living and become "angry young men and women."* The Amplified Bible's translation of this verse sets its meaning in clear focus. It says, "Fathers, do not irritate and provoke your children to anger—*do not* exasperate them to resentment." Note particularly the words "exasperate" and "resentment." What we are to avoid is exasperating our children to the point of deep and abiding resentment.

   c. *One very enlightening cross reference for this phrase is found in Colossians 3:21.* As translated by the Amplified Bible it reads, "Fathers, do not provoke or irritate or fret your children—do not be hard on them or harass them; lest they become discouraged and sullen and morose and feel inferior and frustrated; do

122

not break their spirit." The New American Standard Bible translates the same verse, "Fathers, do not exasperate your children, that they may not lose heart." The Greek word rendered "they may lose heart" by the New American Standard Bible or "break their spirit" by the Amplified Bible literally means "to take the wind out of their sails." God is saying, "Don't raise your children in such a way as to take the wind out of their sails. Don't raise your children in such a way that they become utterly frustrated, cast down, bitter, hostile, lazy, pessimistic, negativistic, fearful, frightened, insecure, rebellious, resentful, ungodly, and wayward young people."

2. *"By all means,"* God says, *"avoid provoking your children to wrath."* But how do we fulfill this injunction? How do we avoid provoking our children to wrath? I offer the following suggestions as a partial answer to that question. To avoid provoking our children to wrath:

   a. *We must not expect more of them than they are capable of giving or doing* (Prov. 22:6; I Cor. 13:11; Gen. 33:12-14). Do not underestimate, but do not overestimate their capabilities (Rom. 12:3).

   b. *We need to be careful about the way that we reprimand or correct them.*

      1) Proverbs 15:1; Ephesians 4:31; Matthew 18:15; I Timothy 5:1, 2 describe the respectful and courteous way we should deal with children as well as adults. Yet how frequently we talk to children in a tone of voice or in a way we would never talk to adults.

      2) One man told me that when he was a child his father made a habit of calling him "dumb" or "stupid." To this day, though he is a very intelligent man with a very responsible position, he still thinks of himself as "dumb" or "stupid."

      3) When speaking to your children, avoid using words like these: "When will you ever . . . ?" "If your head weren't attached. . . ." "You always. . . ." "You never. . . ." "You dummy." "You clumsy ox." "You slob." You knucklehead." Words such as these can be lethal weapons, leaving damaging scars on your children. If you have been accustomed to speaking to your children in this way, apologize and ask for forgiveness, and seek to reassure them that you do love and respect them.

   c. *We must practice what we preach. We must avoid double standards* (Phil. 4:9; I Cor. 11:1; Matt. 23:1-4; Deut. 6:4-9). Children are quick to spot insincerity and hypocrisy. They resent it deeply.

d. *We ought to impregnate the minds of our children with proper values and standards by precept and personal example.*
   1) Our society has made idols out of power, strength, beauty, wealth, intelligence, and athletic ability. These are the things that people value.
   2) In our society a successful person is someone who possesses at least one of these things. A really successful person is someone who has several of these things. An unsuccessful man is someone who has none of these assets.
   3) According to the Bible, this way of measuring worth and success is wrong. These are not the things that God values most. These are not the most important things in life. We must, therefore, labor to instill in our children's minds the fact that we do not value them on the basis of these external, superficial qualities (I Sam. 16:7; I Pet. 3:3, 4). The child who is not as intelligent or handsome or athletically inclined must know that we love him and value him just as much as we do the child who possesses these qualities. (I Cor. 12:23 contains an important principle on this issue.)
e. *We should seek to have many good times with our children.*
   1) Building up a memory bank of happy experiences will engender a good attitude toward you and provide the needed cement in your relationship when you must correct, rebuke, or chastise your children.
   2) Often a remembrance of the fun that they have had with you will help them to realize that you are not an ogre or a sour puss who enjoys being nasty and mean (Ps. 128; Prov. 5:15-18; Eccles. 3:4; Luke 15:17-24; Prov. 15:13; 17:22).
f. *We should freely communicate love and appreciation to them* (I Cor. 13:1-8; 16:14; John 13:34, 35; I Thess. 2:7, 8).
   1) Make it a practice frequently to manifest your love and appreciation to your children in a tangible form.
   2) Do this in many ways—by a hug, a kiss, a pat on the shoulder, by words, by a note, by a gift, by playing with them, by listening to them, by respecting their opinions.
g. *We ought to allow them to fail, to make mistakes, to have faults without jumping all over them and giving them the impression that they are not accepted unless they are perfect* (Eph. 4:1, 2; Col. 3:12-14; I Pet. 4:8; II Tim. 2:24, 25). Home, for the child, must be a safe place; a place where he will be understood and helped, a place where people will not mock him or make fun of his faults and weaknesses, a place where people may disagree with him but still welcome and respect him, a place where

people will encourage him and bind up his wounds, a place where people really care about him.

h. *We should make our expectations, rules, and regulations known to them.*

1) God makes His expectations for us very clear in His Word. We do not need to be in the dark concerning His desire for us.

2) In similar fashion, we should deal with our children. Not knowing what their parents expect of them can be an alarming, frustrating experience for children. When this happens, they are never sure that they are doing what they should be doing. Nor are they certain that they will not be whacked or yelled at for not doing something they did not know they should be doing. Children are not mind readers. Limits and expectations must be clearly delineated. Their presence provides security and structure. Their absence encourages insecurity, frustration, hostility, and resentment. (Study the book of Proverbs where a father makes his counsel and expectations for his children known.)

i. *We ought to admit our mistakes to them, ask forgiveness when we have failed them, and seek to make restitution* (James 5:16; Matt. 5:23, 24; Prov. 16:2; 21:2).

j. *We need to make it easy and desirable for them to approach us with their problems, difficulties, and concerns.*

1) Learn to be a good listener when your children want to talk. Be available to them as much as possible. Give them your undivided attention unless it is infeasible.

2) Avoid being a mind reader or an interrupter or a critic. Stir yourself up to be really interested in what interests your children. They can tell when you are actually listening or just pretending. If you do not give them your undivided attentention or if you constantly put them off when they want to talk, they will soon not even try to talk to you. In their minds, you are not interested in them anyway. Such a state of affairs is very devastating to your relationship with your children. But even more important than that, such a state of affairs may hinder you from fulfilling your God-given parental goal. Ephesians 6:4 says that the goal of parents for their children should be to bring them up in the Lord. It also indicates that to do that we must avoid provoking them to wrath. This is the first part of God's strategy for effective child raising.

B. A second part of God's strategy for bringing up children is found in the words "bring them up in the admonition or instruction of the Lord."

1. Literally, the Greek word translated "admonition" or "instruction" means "to put in the mind" or "to place on the mind."
   a. Parents, therefore, are to bring their children up by putting something in or on their minds.
   b. And what is it that they are to put in their children's minds? Why, it is the instruction, counsel, or admonition of the Lord which is found in the Word of God.
   c. Jay Adams has said that this means that a child "must be reached in his heart with God's Word. It is this message that speaks of a loving Lord who came and gave Himself for His people which first must touch our children's hearts, bringing them to repentance and faith. Parents must lead them to repentance, lead them to conviction of sin, and bring them to the Savior. And then they must continue to show them what He wants and continue to motivate them . . ." (*Christian Living in the Home,* p. 122).
2. *God has something to say about all areas of truth and life in His Word.*
   a. In His Word, God makes important statements about God and man, about sin and salvation, about the person and work of Jesus Christ, about the person and work of the Holy Spirit, about heaven and hell, about creation and providence, about angels and demons, about the past, present, and future, about regeneration, election, redemption, salvation, repentance, and faith, about sanctification, and about a host of other theological doctrines. Our children need to know these doctrines. And *it is our privilege and responsibility as parents to expound these doctrines to them according to our understanding and their capacity to receive them.*
   b. But in the Bible God not only makes important statements about deep theological doctrines; *He also gives instruction and principles to guide us in every area of life.* In the Bible, God gives us principles to help us to know how to relate to other people, how to control and use our emotions, how to use our time and money, how to face and solve problems, how to make decisions, how to overcome sinful anger, bitterness, and resentment, how to have a good marriage, how to make friends, how to respond to mistreatment, how to work, how to become an effective communicator, how to dress, how to be good parents, how to establish proper values and standards, how to pray, how to study the Bible, and how to do a host of other things. The Bible is the most practical book in the world, and *it is our privilege and responsibility to bring our children up by placing these truths in their minds.*

126

3. Now I am not saying that we must personally do all the instructing.
   a. Indeed, *we may and should use all of the resources of the church* and even Christian people outside of our church to help us do our job. We may and should put good Christian literature into the hands of our children. We may send our children to a Christian school where biblical training will be given every school day.
   b. But though we may use all of these resources, we must realize that *the ultimate responsibility for bringing up our children to know the Scriptures rests not with the church or school but with us as parents, and especially with those of us who are fathers.* We as parents are responsible to bring up our children by placing in their minds the admonition, the counsel, the instruction, the correction of the Word of God.
      1) *It is by the Scriptures that men are made wise unto salvation through Jesus Christ* (II Tim. 3:15). "Faith comes by hearing the message, and the message is heard through the Word of Christ" (Rom. 10:17).
      2) *It is by the Scripture* that men are taught, reproved, corrected, trained in righteousness, *made mature*, and thoroughly equipped for every good work (II Tim. 3:16, 17).
      3) God's means of saving people and making those people like Jesus Christ (mature) is through the admonition and instruction of the Word of God. If, therefore, we as parents honestly want to bring our children up to spiritual maturity, *we must see to it that the truth of God's Word is placed in their minds.* If possible, we should try to give our children a good academic education. But even more important than that, we must train them in the counsel and admonition of the Word of God. We must train them by formal and informal instruction, by precept and principle and illustration, but especially by our own practical, consistent, godly example. This is a second part of God's strategy for raising children. It cannot be ignored without doing harm to our children.
C. A third part of God's strategy for bringing up children is contained in the words "bring them up in the discipline of the Lord."
   1. Contrary to what some people think—mostly those who do not have any children of their own or who are not around children very much —children are not little angels.
      a. As we noted earlier, Scripture asserts that "a child left to himself brings shame to his mother" (Prov. 29:15).
      b. This happens because "foolishness is bound up in the heart of a child" (Prov. 22:15). They "are by nature children of wrath"

(Eph. 2:3). They "are estranged (from God and righteousness) from the womb" (Ps. 58:3; 51:5).

   c. Children do not naturally do what is right, nor do they eagerly choose what is good and holy. Indeed, the very opposite is true.

2. Consequently, to help them make the right choices and learn to do the right things and live the right way, *God says they need to be disciplined.*

   a. Discipline refers to enforced learning, or learning with structure, or *learning with some teeth in it.*

   b. God says, "If you want your children to grow up right, you are going to have to make it wise for them to obey. There will be times when they will be opposed to the things that are for their own good. Then you will have to use discipline to motivate them to do the right thing."

3. It is important to notice that *there is only one kind of discipline that we should use in bringing up our children.* We are to bring our children up *"in the discipline of the Lord."*

   a. *The discipline of the Lord is the discipline which is taught in the Bible.* A perusal of the book of Proverbs reveals that it is replete with practical instructions concerning this matter. So the discipline of the Lord would be the kind of discipline commanded by the book of Proverbs. That great book does not merely contain some man's ideas of discipline, but God's truth about proper discipline.

   b. Still further, *the discipline of the Lord refers to the kind of discipline that God uses with His children.* Hebrews 12 indicates that God disciplines every person who is truly His child by faith in Jesus Christ.

   c. Keeping these two thoughts in mind, we conclude that *bringing our children up in the discipline of the Lord means that we use on our children the kind of discipline that God uses with Christians or the kind that He commends in His Word.*

4. Because of the abundance of biblical material on the subject of discipline, we cannot deal with it in an exhaustive manner in this manual. The following list is presented only as a sketchy outline of some principles which I think are involved in the exercise of God's kind of discipline.

   a. *Clear boundaries and limits need to be set for the children* (Prov. 29:15; Ex. 20:1-17).

   b. *Avoid the danger of unannounced rules.*

   c. *Make sure the children understand your rules and regulations.* Write out the ones that are continuing rules for them. Ask the children to explain to you what they think your rules mean.

d. *Do not give your children too many rules.* (Compare Ex. 20:1-17; Matt. 22:34-40.)
e. *Avoid making hard and fast rules about trivial things.*
f. *Do not make rules that your children cannot keep.*
g. *Beware of constantly moving the boundaries or changing the rules and regulations.* If this happens frequently, your child will become insecure and begin to doubt the validity of all your rules. God is consistent, and we should be also.
h. *Do not fall into the practice of making arbitrary rules.* As much as possible explain your reason for the rules you make. (Very small children, of course, are an exception to this suggestion.) God is not obligated to give reasons for what He asks us to do, and yet He often does (note Eph. 6:1, 2). Do not allow your children to argue disrespectfully about your reasons. After stating your reasons, they may still not agree. Nevertheless, they will know you are not acting arbitrarily or capriciously.
i. *Seek to establish your rules and regulations on biblical principles.*
j. *Remember that rules and regulations are for the good of your children.* They need boundaries to give them security, to help them learn right and wrong. They will never become disciplined people, disciples of Christ, without structure to their lives.
k. *Do not make rules which you know you cannot enforce.*
l. *Whenever possible, not only tell them what you expect, but show them.*
m. *Impart the idea that you expect immediate obedience.*
n. *When the rules are broken, administer the necessary chastisement.*
   1) *While the children are young, the primary (though not the only) means of chastisement will be the literal rod.* (Compare Prov. 13:24; 22:15; 23:13, 14; 29:15). The rod is a merciful form of discipline, because it is quickly administered. The lesson is learned swiftly, hugs and kisses can come immediately, reconciliation and restoration to normal relations is experienced with hardly any delay.
   2) There are, however, other legitimate kinds of discipline. *Sometimes another form of discipline which is more in keeping with a particular act of disobedience may be the wisest procedure.* God does not always spank us in exactly the same way. IIe suits the chastisement to our need.
   3) *Chastisement should be administered with instruction* (Prov. 29:15).
   4) *Chastisement should be administered corporately.* The children should know that mother and father agree. If they get the idea that one parent is an "easy touch" and the other is

a "hard-liner," the results can be disastrous.

5) *Discipline should be administered consistently.* We should not be the kind of parents who punish the children for something on one occasion and then ignore it when they do the same thing on another occasion. Discipline will not produce growth and correction unless it is consistent. If an action is wrong once, it is wrong the second, third, and tenth time unless, of course, you realize your standard was erroneous.

6) *Chastisement should be administered with enough force to make it inadvisable to disobey again.* Discipline should be hard enough to be remembered, but not so hard that the children are damaged (Prov. 23:13, 14).

7) *Discipline should be administered out of a heart of love* (Prov. 13:24; I Cor. 16:14; Rev. 3:19). Incidentally, love and anger are not necessarily opposites (note Eph. 4:26, 32). Uncontrolled, sinful anger and love are very incompatible (Eph. 4:31, 32; I Cor. 13:4). However, controlled anger against sin and genuine love may dwell in the same heart at the same time and be directed toward the same person. It is legitimate for us to be angry with our children over genuine disobedience. At the same time, we must not express that anger in sinful ways (yelling, screaming, nastiness, irritation, etc.) but in loving ways for the good of our children.

5. Remember, the Scripture says, "A child left to himself brings shame to his mother." But more than that, a child left to himself, without discipline, will not naturally and automatically grow up and become like Jesus Christ. "Oh no," God says, "for that to happen children need to be brought up in the discipline of the Lord."

IV. Conclusion.

A. Well, there you have a biblical philosophy of child raising. A biblical philosophy of child raising means that:

1. Dad is to be the final authority in the home.

2. The main goal for parents in reference to children is to bring the children to maturity in Christ.

3. Parents should avoid those things that exasperate their children and provoke them to wrath; they should attempt to bring their children up in the discipline and instruction of the Lord.

B. Now that is a biblical philosophy of child raising, and I commend it to you as the one you should adopt for your family.

1. First and foremost, you ought to raise your children this way because this is God's plan for raising children. If you are a Christian, your God and Savior commands you to raise your children this way. To fail to comply is disobedience to your God.

130

2. Secondly, you ought to commit yourself to this plan because it will be good for your entire family. It will be good for the wife, the husband, and the children.

3. Thirdly, you ought to commit yourself to this plan because, if you do, your children will no longer be a wedge that drives you and your mate apart but a bond that unites you together even more closely. God's revealed purpose for your marriage is that the two of you become one flesh. You are to experience oneness in every area of life, and that includes the area of children. And you can develop genuine unity in your child raising effort by mutually adopting and seeking to implement God's plan for raising children. Remember, it is not just one of many ways. It is the only way for a Christian to go.

SUPPLEMENTARY READING FOR UNIT 7

Christian Living in the Home, Jay Adams, chapters 1 and 8.
Competent to Counsel, Jay Adams, Presbyterian and Reformed Publishing Co., Nutley, N. J., 1970, pp. 188-220.
The Christian Home in a Changing World, Gene Getz, chapters 5-11.
Reformation for the Family, ed. Erroll Hulse, chapters 1, 4, 18.
Withhold Not Correction, Bruce Ray, Mack Publishing Co., Cherry Hill, N. J., 1973.
The Christian Home, Shirley Rice, lessons 11-22.

DISCUSSION AND STUDY QUESTIONS FOR UNIT 7
DEVELOPING UNITY THROUGH A COMMON PHILOSOPHY OF CHILD RAISING

To be completed together by husband and wife.

A. List several character traits which you think parents should seek to develop in their children.

1. _____

2. _____

3. _____

4. _____

5. _____

6. _____

7. _____

8. _____

B. List some areas many parents emphasize that you think should not be emphasized.

   1. Money
   2. Clothing
   3. _____
   4. _____
   5. _____
   6. _____
   7. _____

C. Look up the following verses, and see what character traits God wants children to have.

   1. Ephesians 6:1 _____
   2. Ephesians 6:2 _____
   3. I John 4:7 _____
   4. Philippians 2:4 _____
   5. Matthew 22:37 _____
   6. Acts 20:35 _____
   7. Ephesians 4:25 _____
   8. II Corinthians 8:21 _____
   9. Proverbs 12:22 _____
   10. Hebrews 11:6 _____

11. Galatians 5:22, 23 _____

12. Luke 2:52 _____

13. Proverbs 1:5 _____

14. Proverbs 23:12 _____

15. Judges 13:24 _____

16. I Samuel 2:26 _____

17. Ephesians 4:26, 27 _____

18. Ephesians 4:32 _____

19. Proverbs 12:24; 13:4 _____

20. Proverbs 13:3 _____

21. Proverbs 16:5; 17:19; 18:12 _____

22. Proverbs 17:17 _____

23. Proverbs 16:32 _____

D. Evaluate your children in the light of the list compiled under question C.

    Name of Child   *Areas of Greatest Need*

    Child 1. _____   a. _____

                           b. _____

                           c. _____

                           d. _____

                           e. _____

                           f. _____

    Child 2. _____   a. _____

Name of Child	Areas of Greatest Need

b. _____

c. _____

d. _____

e. _____

f. _____

Child 3. _____ a. _____

b. _____

c. _____

d. _____

e. _____

f. _____

Child 4. _____ a. _____

b. _____

c. _____

d. _____

e. _____

f. _____

E. Make a list of steps you will take (things you will do) to develop these godly characteristics in your children. (Study Phil. 4:9; II Tim. 1:5; 3:15; Prov. 1:8-9; 7:1-5; Deut. 6:4-9; Heb. 12:5-11; I Sam. 3:12; Prov. 3:11, 12; I Tim. 4:12; Eccles. 8:11; Eph. 6:4; Prov. 29:15; Josh. 24:15; Gen. 18:19; Deut. 16:11; Ex. 20:8-11.)

1. _____

2. _____

3. _____

4. _____

5. _____

6. _____

7. _____

8. _____

9. _____

10. _____

11. _____

12. _____

F. Study the book of Proverbs and list everything it has to say about parent-child relations. Note where you are failing and seek God's help to change.

1. _____

2. _____

3. _____

4. _____

5. _____

6. _____

7. _____

8. _____

9. _____

135

10. _____

11. _____

12. _____

13. _____

14. _____

15. _____

16. _____

17. _____

18. _____

19. _____

20. _____

21. _____

22. _____

23. _____

24. _____

25. _____

Make your children's needs a matter of primary concern. Examine your own life and seek to be a good example; give proper biblical instruction concerning God's desires and directives; pray that God would help you and your children; ask for forgiveness from God and your children for your failures.

G. Examine the kind of discipline you are giving to your children. Are you really disciplining them—helping them to become disciples or followers of Jesus Christ who practice self control? Discuss and write down your answers to the following questions.

1. What are your children's chores and responsibilities? Do you have a clear picture of what you expect? Do they? *A list* with clear, specific instructions will be very helpful for you and your children.

2. What are your disciplinary rules, penalties, and procedures? Do you know what they are? Do your children? Are they clear? Fair? Announced? Too many? Too few? Arbitrary? Do you administer them consistently, lovingly, with reproof and instruction, in the fear of God? Again, *a list* with clear, specific instructions will be most helpful for you and your children. For discipline to be effective, children should know what is expected of them, what will happen if they do not obey, and why it will happen. The rules should be explained to the children.

They should be asked for suggestions and reactions. If the suggestions seem to be valuable, they should be included in the final draft of this code of conduct. Then the list should be posted in the appropriate places as a reminder to everyone involved. (For further information on the mechanics and theory of making a code of conduct, read *Competent to Counsel,* Jay Adams, pp. 188-220, or *Christian Living in the Home,* pp. 103-125.)

Chores, Responsibilities, Rules	*Method and Procedure of Corrective Discipline*
1. _____	_____
2. _____	_____
3. _____	_____
4. _____	_____
5. _____	_____
6. _____	_____
7. _____	_____
8. _____	_____
9. _____	_____
10. _____	_____

H. Make a list of areas where you and your spouse disagree on discipline. Seek a biblical solution to these conflicts and commit yourself to stand and act as one person.

1. _____

2. _____

3. _____

4. _____

5. _____

6. _____

7. _____

I. List the areas in which you and your mate have been good examples to your children, and then list the areas in which you have been poor examples.

Good Example   *Poor Example*

1. _____   _____

2. _____   _____

3. _____   _____

4. _____   _____

5. _____   _____

J. Select areas in which your spouse has been a good example, and every now and then call your children's attention to one of these good qualities.

1. _____

2. _____

3. _____

4. _____

5. _____

6. _____

7. _____

K. Select the areas in which you want to be a better example, and start to make the effort. Ask your mate to pray with you about the areas in which you want to improve.

1. _____

2. _____

3. _____

4. _____

5. _____

M. Study I Corinthians 13:4-7 and evaluate your relationship to each child in the light of the various ingredients of love.
Example—Am I loving Billy by being longsuffering? When haven't I been? Am I truly kind to him? When haven't I been?
1. List the areas where you have wronged each child.

   a. _____

   b. _____

   c. _____

   d. _____

   e. _____

2. Ask the child's forgiveness where you have wronged him.

3. List the ways you show love to your child.

   a. _____

   b. _____

   c. _____

   d. _____

   e. _____

f. _____

g. _____

N. Make a list of things you appreciate about each child. Express your appreciation.

1. _____

2. _____

3. _____

4. _____

5. _____

6. _____

O. Study Deuteronomy 6:4-9.
   1. List the parental responsibilities mentioned in this passage.

   a. _____

   b. _____

   c. _____

   d. _____

   e. _____

   f. _____

   2. This passage encourages formal and informal, structured and unstructured Christian education.
      a. How do you teach your children Christian doctrine, standards, values, principles in an informal way?

      1) _____

      2) _____

      3) _____

4) _____

5) _____

6) _____

7) _____

8) _____

9) _____

10) _____

b. How do you teach your children the Word of God in a formal or structural way?

1) _____

2) _____

3) _____

4) _____

5) _____

6) _____

7) _____

c. One method of structured teaching is family devotions. Do you have them? If not, why not plan to begin them soon? How will you (or how do you) conduct family devotions? When? Where? What tools will you or do you use? What elements will you or do you include? How can you provide for variety? How will you involve your children? Ask other Christians. Read books. Pray about your devotions. Discuss and evaluate them with your mate. Write down your ideas.

1) _____

2) _____

3) _____

4) _____

5) _____

6) _____

7) _____

8) _____

9) _____

10) _____

P. Study the following list of suggestions for raising children. Discuss them with your mate. Look up the Scripture verses. Evaluate your child raising efforts in the light of this list. Put a circle around the principles where you are weak or failing. Make these areas a matter of prayer and seek to improve with God's help.

The relevance of some of the texts quoted in support of the suggestions will be seen if the analogy of the relationship that Christians have as God's children to their heavenly father is kept in mind (Heb. 12:5-10).

1. Pray for your child before he is born, and continue to pray for him afterward (I Sam. 1:11, 27, 28; Ps. 71:6; Gal. 1:15; II Tim. 1:5).

2. Examine your expectations for your child. Are they realistic? Evaluate them in the light of the Bible (Gen. 33:12-14; I Cor. 13:11; Matt. 18:10).

3. Love him unconditionally (Deut. 7:7; I John 4:19; 4:10).

4. Look for opportunities when you can commend him. Express appreciation to him frequently (Phil. 1:3; I Thess. 1:2; II Thess. 1:3).

5. Seldom criticize without first expressing appreciation for good points (I Cor. 1:3-13).

6. Give him freedom to make decisions where serious issues are not at stake. Your goal should be to bring your child to maturity in Christ and not to dependence on you (Prov. 22:6; Col. 1:27-28; Eph. 4:13-15; 6:4).

7. Do not compare him with others (Gal. 6:4; II Cor. 10:12-13; I Cor. 12:4-11).

8. Never mock him or make fun of him. Do not belittle your child. Beware of calling him dumb or clumsy or stupid (Matt. 7:12; Eph. 4:29-30; Col. 4:6; Prov. 12:18; 16:24).

9. Do not scold him unnecessarily in front of others (Matt. 18:15).

10. Never make threats or promises that you do not intend to keep (Matt. 5:37; James 5:12; Col. 3:9).

142

11. Don't be afraid to say "no" and when you say it mean it (Gen. 18:19; Prov. 29:15; 22:15; I Sam. 3:13).

12. When your child has problems or is a problem, do not overreact, or lose control of yourself. Do not yell or shout or scream at him (Eph. 4:26-27; I Cor. 16:14; II Tim. 2:24-25).

13. Communicate optimism and expectancy. Do not communicate by word or action that you have given up on your child and are resigned to his being a failure (Philem. 21; II Cor. 9:1-2; I Cor. 13:7).

14. Make sure your child knows exactly what is expected of him. Most of the book of Proverbs is specific counsel from a father to his son.

15. Ask his advice. Include him in some of the discussions about family activities (Rom. 1:11-12; II Tim. 4:11; I Tim. 4:12; John 6:5).

16. When you make a mistake with your child, admit it, and ask your child for forgiveness (Matt. 5:23-24; James 5:16).

17. Have family conferences where you discuss:
    a. Aims of the family
    b. Family projects
    c. Vacations
    d. Devotions
    e. Chores
    f. Discipline
    g. Complaints
    h. Suggestions
    i. Problems
    Welcome contributions from your child (Ps. 128; James 1:19).

18. Assess his areas of strength and then encourage him to develop them. Begin with one, and encourage him really to develop in this area (II Tim. 1:6; 4:5; I Pet. 4:10).

19. Give him much tender loving care. Be free in your expression of love by word and deed (I Cor. 13:1-8; 16:14; John 13:34-35; I Thess. 2:7-8).

20. When your child does something well, commend him. Especially let him know when his attitude and effort are what they should be (I Thess. 1:3-10; Phil. 1:3-5; Col. 1:3-4; Eph. 1:15).

21. Be more concerned about Christian attitudes and character than you are about performance or athletic skill or clothing or external beauty or intelligence (I Sam. 16:7; Gal. 5:22-23; I Peter 3:4-5; Prov. 4:23; Matt. 23:25-28).

22. Have a lot of enjoyment with your child. Plan to have many times of fun and many special events with your children. Make a list of things your family can enjoy together (Prov. 5:15-18; Eph. 6:4; Col. 3:21; Eccles. 3:4; Luke 15:22-24; Prov. 15:13; 17:22).

23. Help your child to learn responsibility by administering discipline fairly, consistently, lovingly, and promptly (Prov. 13:24; I Sam. 3:13; Prov. 19:18; Prov. 22:15).

24. Look upon your child as a person growing and developing as well as already a human being. Look upon the task of raising children as a process

which takes many years to complete (Eph. 6:4; Prov. 22:6; Gal. 6:9; I Cor. 15:58; Isa. 28:9-10).

25. Live your convictions consistently. Your children will learn more by observing your example than they will by listening to your words (Deut. 6:4-9; I Thess. 2:10-12; Phil. 4:9; II Tim. 1:5-7).

26. Recognize that you are responsible to prepare your child for life in this world and in the world to come (Eph. 6:4; Deut. 6:4-9; Ps. 78:5-7; II Tim. 3:15-17).

27. Be very sensitive to the needs, feelings, fears, and opinions of your child (Matt. 18:10; Col. 3:21).

28. Treat the child as though he is important to you and accepted by you (Matt. 18:5-6).

29. Avoid the use of angry or exasperated words (Prov. 15:1; Eph. 4:31-32).

30. Maintain the practice of daily Bible reading, discussions, and prayer (Deut. 6:4-9; II Tim. 3:15; Eph. 6:4; Ps. 1:1-30; 78:5-8; 119:9-11).

31. Become thoroughly involved as a family in a biblical church (Heb. 10: 24-25; Eph. 4:11-16).

32. Make your home a center of Christian hospitality, where your child will be brought into frequent contact with many Christians (Rom. 12:13; Heb. 13:1-2; II Kings 4:8-37).

33. Make it easy for your child to approach you with problems, difficulties, and concerns. Learn to be a good listener. When he needs you, give your child your undivided attention. Avoid being a mind reader or an interrupter or a critic. Show an interest in whatever interests your child, but seek to guide those interests aright. Make yourself available when your child needs you—even if you are busy (James 1:19-20; 3:13-18; Isa. 3:16-18; I Cor. 9:19-23; Phil. 2:3-4).

34. Seek to bring your child to a saving knowledge of Jesus Christ. Labor to bring your child to Christ. Become all things to your child that you might win your child for Christ. God, of course, must do the saving, bring conviction, give repentance and faith. You, however, may provide the environment in which God saves by your prayers, godly speech and example, daily devotions, and involvement in a sound biblical church (II Tim. 3: 14-17; II Tim. 1:5-7; Eph. 6:4; Deut. 6:4-9; Mark 10:13-14; Rom. 10: 13-17; I Cor. 1:18-21).

This list of principles is available in pamphlet form from Christian Counseling Center, 1 Lakeside Plaza, Lake Charles, Louisiana 70601. Ask for the pamphlet, "How to Grow a Child for God." Specify the number desired. You will be billed for the nominal cost.

Q. A few more questions for discussion.
1. Why do you want to have children?
2. How many children do you want? When? How far apart?

3. What should be your primary objectives in raising children?
4. What are your family goals?
5. What are the greatest problems parents face in raising children?
6. What projects could you become involved in as a family?
7. How can your family minister effectively to your friends and neighbors?
8. What can you do to develop stronger family relations? To become better friends?
9. How can you provide for quality times when you can be alone with each other as well as well for quality times with the children?
10. Discuss the matter of a family standard. How do you decide what is right and wrong for your family?
11. How can parents develop maturity in children and prepare them to leave while at the same time guiding them properly?
12. How did your parents differ in their child raising concepts from the parents of your mate? Are your concepts a reaction against your parents' concepts or an extension of your parents' concepts? Have you seriously examined your concepts to see if they are biblical?
13. How can you make your home a fun place, a place of refuge and safety where your children will like to be?

UNIT 8

Promoting and Maintaining Unity in Marriage by Means of Family Religion

A. Describe what the following verses have to say about family religion.

1. Genesis 18:19 ―――――――――――――――――――

2. Exodus 12:21, 24-28 ――――――――――――――――

3. Exodus 20:8-10 ――――――――――――――――――

4. II Samuel 6:20 ―――――――――――――――――――

5. Joshua 24:15 ――――――――――――――――――――

6. Acts 16:15 ―――――――――――――――――――――

7. Acts 21:8, 9 ―――――――――――――――――――――

8. I Corinthians 16:15 ―――――――――――――――――

9. II Timothy 4:19 ―――――――――――――――――――

10. Romans 16:10-13 ――――――――――――――――――

B. State how the following verses suggest a family may serve God together.

1. Deuteronomy 16:11, 14 ―――――――――――――――

2. Deuteronomy 29:10, 11 ―――――――――――――――

3. Joshua 8:34, 35 ――――――――――――――――――

4. Acts 10:24-33 ――――――――――――――――――――

5. Romans 16:15 ―――――――――――――――――――――

6. I Corinthians 16:15 ―――――――――――――――――

146

7. Acts 18:24-28 _____

8. III John 1-6 _____

9. Mark 2:14, 15 _____

10. Hebrews 13:2 _____

11. Matthew 25:34-36 _____

12. I Peter 3:7 _____

C. Make a list of the ways that your family will serve Christ.

1. _____

2. _____

3. _____

4. _____

5. _____

6. _____

7. _____

8. _____

9. _____

10. _____

D. Plan when and how you will begin (timing and strategy).

1. *When?* Date   *Activity*

a. _____   _____

b. _____   _____

c. _____   _____

d. _____   _____

e. _____   _____

f. _____   _____

g. _____   _____

2. How?

   a. Activity   Strategy

   _____   _____

                      _____

                      _____

                      _____

                      _____

                      _____

   b. Activity   Strategy

   _____   _____

                      _____

                      _____

                      _____

                      _____

                      _____

   c. Activity   Strategy

   _____   _____

                      _____

148

_____

_____

_____

_____

d. Activity   Strategy

_____   _____

                            _____

                            _____

                            _____

                            _____

149

Conclusion

Marriage is a unique human relationship. Good friend-to-friend relationships are beautiful and rewarding experiences. Good parent-child relationships are emphasized throughout the Scripture by precept, illustration, and example. But, according to the Word of God, no other human relationship should receive the attention or provide the satisfaction that marriage does.

Marriage was ordained by God as a unique relationship for unique purposes to provide unique fulfillment in the context of a unique intimacy. "For this cause shall a man leave his father and mother, and shall cleave to his wife, and *they shall become one flesh"* (Gen. 2:24).

God's stated purpose for marriage is deep, total unity, and it can become a glorious reality in the here and now.

1. It won't happen *all at once.* It is a deepening and expanding experience.

2. It won't happen *once for all.* All inter-personal relationships have their ebbs and flows and require continuous effort and attention.

3. It won't happen merely by an exertion of your own will power. Perhaps you have already discovered this. Perhaps you have studied this manual and tried to implement what you have learned, but failed. Maybe you are ready to say that it all sounds very good, but it's impossible.

Well, if that's what you think, you are right, for it is absolutely impossible for any man or woman to experience genuine, biblical oneness apart from the regenerating, sanctifying power of Jesus Christ. By nature we are proud, stubborn, rebellious, weak, and selfish (Jer. 17:9; Mark 7:21-22; Rom. 3:10-23; 5:6; 8: 3-8). We are sinners by practice; we are sinners by nature. We have a bad record before God; we have a sinful, selfish heart. We turn to our own way as naturally as rain falls from heaven or fire burns (Isa. 53:6).

And this is one reason why Jesus Christ came into the world; why He lived and died and rose again. He died the just for the unjust that He might bring us to God (I Pet. 3:18). He died in the place of those who truly trust Him, taking the punishment of their sins. He lived in their place, keeping God's law perfectly as their substitute. Because of His life and death in their place, sinners who trust in Him are reconciled. They become one with God (Rom. 5:6-11).

But something else happens when a person sincerely believes on the Lord Jesus Christ. That person receives the gift of the Holy Spirit (Eph. 1:13, 14; I Cor. 6:19, 20), who enables him to live in a manner, to relate to people in a way that was previously impossible and to obey God and fulfill His Word. "Walk in (or by) the Spirit, and you will not fulfill the lust of the flesh" (Gal. 5:16). Walk by the Spirit, and your lives will not be governed by the standards and according to the dictates of your flesh, but controlled by the Holy Spirit (Rom. 8:4).

As we depend upon Him, as we rely upon Him, as we obey Him, the Holy

Spirit gives us power to do what we could never do in our own strength. He brings our sinful thoughts, desires, and reasonings into captivity and enables us to be obedient to Jesus Christ (II Cor. 10:4, 5).

As we trust Him, rely upon him, and seek to obey Him, He enables us to become the husbands and wives the Bible says we should be. He empowers us to implement the biblical precepts and principles which we have learned through this manual.

By His power a husband and wife can right here and now to a large extent:

1. Understand and implement the complementary roles and responsibilities of the husband and wife;

2. Develop and maintain a good communication system;

3. View and use money according to a biblical perspective;

4. Experience mutually satisfying sex relations;

5. Raise their children according to the precepts of the Word of God;

6. Understand and implement God's overall purpose for marriage stated in Genesis 2:18-25.

By His power, the impossible can happen—one plus one can really equal one.